MAKING BIRDHOUSES
Easy and Advanced Projects

GLADSTONE CALIFF

DOVER PUBLICATIONS, INC.
Mineola, New York

Bibliographical Note

This Dover edition, first published in 2005, is a somewhat altered republication of *Permanent Bird Houses*, originally published by The Bruce Publishing Company, Milwaukee, Wisconsin, 1924. For the Dover edition, the original introduction, acknowledgment, sections on stucco houses, sparrow traps, and birdhouse contests, as well as the index, have been dropped. A supplement of 20 plates from *Boy Bird House Architecture*, by Leon H. Baxter, published by The Bruce Publishing Company, Milwaukee, Wisconsin, in 1920, has been added under the title "Easy Projects for Beginners."

International Standard Book Number

ISBN-13: 978-0-486-44183-2
ISBN-10: 0-486-44183-0

Manufactured in the United States by Courier Corporation
44183006   2014
www.doverpublications.com

*This book is affectionately dedicated to the
memory of my Mother.*

"The little bird sits at his door in the sun
 Atilt, like a blossom among the leaves,
 And lets his illumined being o'errun
 With the deluge of summer it receives:
 His mate feels the eggs beneath her wings,
 And the heart in her dumb breast flutters and sings:
 He sings to the wide world, and she to her nest
 In the nice ear of nature which song is the best."

From *The Vision of Sir Launfal*, Lowell.

Publisher's Note

Besides adding color and beauty to our gardens, wild birds consume vast quantities of weed seeds, harmful insects, and other pests. For these reasons many people like to feed and provide homes for the birds. This book shows you how to construct a variety of homes specially designed to appeal to such species as bluebirds, wrens, purple martins, woodpeckers, robins, nuthatches, tree swallows, chickadees, and others.

Here you'll find measurements and construction diagrams for building both simple and elaborate homes—from a one-room wren house to a forty-two-room martin house. You'll learn what kind of woods and other materials to use, along with such essentials as ventilation, cleaning, where and how to hang or place the birdhouse, and how to discourage cats and other predators. The author also provides plans for bird feeders, observation houses, and shows how to make birdhouses out of such nontraditional materials as tin cans, coconuts, and gourds.

Some of these projects are challenging enough to satisfy the experienced woodworker, while a special supplement (pp. 57–80) includes eighteen houses ideal for the beginning birdhouse builder. Whatever your skill level, you're sure to find a suitable project here, one that will provide hours of entertainment and rewarding activity. Best of all, while you're enjoying this fun and satisfying hobby, you'll be helping birds survive and flourish in suburban backyards, farmyards, city lots, parks, orchards, and other environments.

Table of Contents

(con't)

TABLE OF CONTENTS (CON'T.)

EASY PROJECTS FOR BEGINNERS

PERMANENT BIRD HOUSES

BIRDHOUSE CONSTRUCTION

Before building a birdhouse, the maker should have in mind the kind of house he is going to make; whether it is for martins, bluebirds, or wrens. An architect, when planning a house, must know whom he is working for, the size of the family and the particular taste of the occupants. The same applies to birdhouses.

ESSENTIALS OF A BIRDHOUSE

1. House built for certain kind of bird.
2. Correct amount of floor space.
3. Proper depth of house.
4. Right sized entrance, proper distance from floor.
5. Arrangements for cleaning.
6. Means provided for ventilation.
7. Good exterior finish.
8. Smooth interior, free from nails.
9. Good construction, tight joints.
10. Quarter-inch hole bored in floor of house for escape of moisture.

If it is desired to make a house practical, it must be built for a certain type of bird. A house that would suit a family of martins would not suit a family of wrens. Each bird builds a different kind of nest which varies in size and shape.

CONSTRUCTION

The house should be built of good material to make it durable. Cypress, poplar and white pine are excellent materials. They are cheap in price, easy to work, and weather well. The joints should be tight to prevent drafts. Nails and screws should be set in and puttied over. Birdhouses should be built with the idea of giving the birds forty years of service.

FINISHING BIRDHOUSES

The birdhouses described in this book may be finished as follows: A martin house may be painted white as that has proved to be a satisfactory color. The paint protects the wood and the birds take to this color. A number of martin houses finished with white paint by the author were all occupied. An old established firm that specializes in the manufacture of birdhouses finishes martin houses with white paint. Martins will also build in rustic houses.

Bluebirds will build in a house that is finished in brown, gray, or green. They prefer these colors to any other. They also like rustic houses.

The wren will build in a house of most any color. The colors, brown, gray and green are recommended because they blend with the landscape and do not make the house so conspicuous. The wren will build in anything from a coat pocket to an empty shoe.

Rustic houses, made by nailing bark on the outside, generally prove unsatisfactory. A house made in this fashion draws and holds dampness, and the bark becomes worm-eaten and drops off, lasting but a season or two. Do not confuse this type of house with natural wood boxes. Natural wood boxes are made from a hollow branch or some part of a tree and are covered with natural bark. This type of house generally weathers well and makes an excellent home for birds preferring rustic houses. Any type of bird box can be made rustic by staining the outside dark and applying two or three coats of spar varnish.

DON'TS FOR BIRDHOUSE BUILDERS

1. Don't place a martin house in or near a tree or other obstruction. It may be placed from fifteen to fifty feet in the air, situated so as to allow the martins to circle.

2. Don't make the porches on a martin house too narrow.

3. Don't make the opening in a wren house less than $\frac{7}{8}$" in diameter. It should be the size of a quarter of a dollar. English sparrows cannot force themselves through such an opening.

4. Don't build a house unless some way is provided for cleaning and ventilating it.

5. Don't paint the inside of a birdhouse.

6. Don't fail to cover the entrance to a martin house with cardboard or screen after the martins leave in the late summer. Open again at the date of arrival in the spring. This keeps the sparrows from using the building for winter sleeping quarters and eventually building their nests before the martins have time to establish themselves.

7. Don't make the perches square. A round perch is superior.

8. Don't place a house made of tin or with a tin roof directly in the sun. Better build with wood.

9. Don't have ventilating holes lower than the entrance.

10. Don't make the entrance on a level with the floor, as the young birds are in danger of falling from the nest.

11. Don't place the houses too close together.

12. Don't have more than one entrance to each room.

13. Don't place a railing around the porch of a martin house.

14. Don't leave the inside of the house rough. It should be smooth and free from nail points.

15. Don't fail to bore a quarter inch hole in the floor of each house to allow the escape of moisture.

16. Don't make the perch on a wren house too long. It should be short to prevent larger birds from standing on the perch and attacking the young in the nest.

(continued on page 22)

PLATE I

JUSTAMERE
WREN HOUSE

BILL OF MATERIAL

4 PC $\frac{1}{4}" \times 3\frac{1}{4}" \times 6\frac{1}{2}"$ SIDES
1 PC $\frac{1}{4}" \times 4\frac{3}{4}" \times 5\frac{1}{4}"$ BOTTOM
1 PC $\frac{1}{4}" \times 5\frac{3}{4}" \times 6\frac{1}{4}"$ TOP
1 PC $\frac{1}{4}" \times 3\frac{3}{4}" \times 4\frac{1}{4}"$ "
1 PC $\frac{1}{4}" \times 1\frac{5}{8}" \times 2\frac{1}{4}"$ "
1 PC $\frac{3}{4}" \times 1" \times 2\frac{1}{4}"$ NECK
1 PC $\frac{1}{4}" \times 1\frac{3}{8}" \times 1\frac{5}{8}"$ CAP
1 PC $\frac{1}{4}" \times 1\frac{1}{2}"$ ROUND PERCH
4 $\frac{3}{4}"$ #4 FLAT HEAD SCREWS

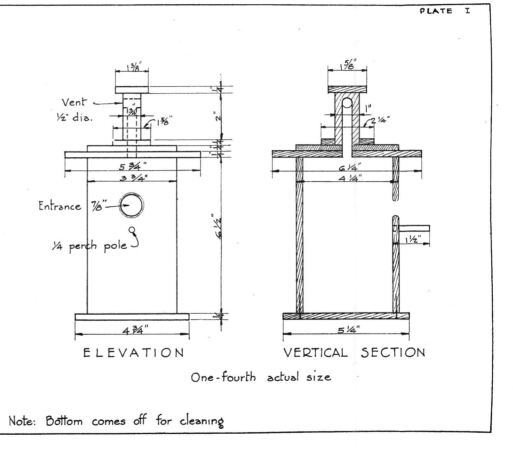

ELEVATION   VERTICAL SECTION

One-fourth actual size

Note: Bottom comes off for cleaning

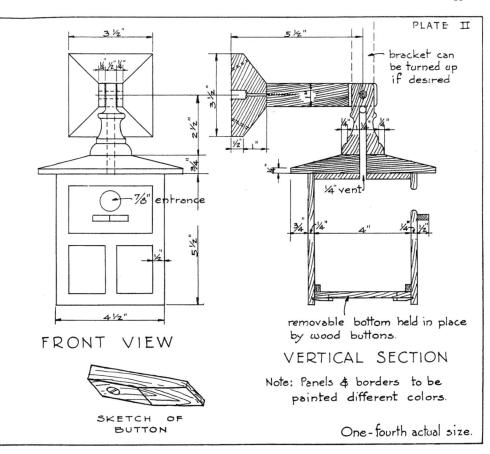

PLATE II

3 ½"

5 ½"

bracket can
be turned up
if desired

¼ ½ ¼

3 ½"

2 ½"

½"   1"

¾"

7/8" entrance

¼ vent

¼   ¼   ¼

5 ½"

½"

¾"   ¼"   4"   ¼" ½"

4 ½"

FRONT VIEW

removable bottom held in place
by wood buttons.

VERTICAL SECTION

Note: Panels & borders to be
painted different colors.

One-fourth actual size.

THE LANTERN
WREN HOUSE

BILL OF MATERIAL

2	PC	¼" x 4" x 5 ½"		SIDES
2	PC	¼" x 4 ½" x 5 ½"		"
1	PC	¼" x 4" x 4"		BOTTOM
2	PC	¼" x ¼" x 4"		STOPS
1	PC	¼" x 4" x 4"		TOP
1	PC	¾" x 6" x 6"		"
1	PC	1 ½" x 3 ½" x 3 ½"		BRACKET
1	PC	1" x 1" x 5"		ARM
1	PC	¼" x 1 ½" x ½"		PERCH
1	PC	¼" x 1"		DOWEL
1	TURNING			
1	2" SCREW #14			
2	WOODEN BUTTONS			

SKETCH OF
BUTTON

CORNER WREN HOUSE

BILL OF MATERIAL

2	PC	½" x 7¾" x 7¾" x 11"	TOP & BOTTOM
1	PC	½" x 5½" x 8"	BACK
1	PC	½" x 6" x 8"	"
1	PC	½" x 9½" x 8"	FRONT
2	PC	11"	COVE MOLD
1	PC	¼" x 2¼" ROUND	PERCH
6	½" SCREWS		

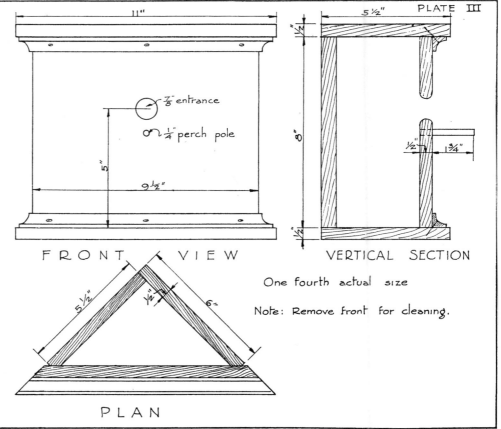

11"

⅞" entrance

¼" perch pole

5"

9½"

FRONT VIEW

PLAN

5½"

½"

6"

5½"

PLATE III

⅛"

8"

½"

1¾"

½"

VERTICAL SECTION

One fourth actual size

Note: Remove front for cleaning.

PLATE IV

CATHEDRAL
WREN HOUSE
BILL OF MATERIAL

1 PC	½" x 4" x 4"	BOTTOM
4 PC	¾" x ¾" x 4"	RAIL
4 PC	¾" x ¾" x 6½"	SPIRES
2 PC	½" x 4" x 3½"	SIDES
2 PC	½" x 4" x 5½"	ENDS
1 PC	½" x 3¼" x 5"	ROOF
1 PC	½" x 3¾" x 5"	"
1 PC	½" x 2" x 5½"	HANGER
1 PC	½" x 1" x 2"	PERCH
1 PC	½" x 1½" x 1½"	HOOD
1 PC	½" x 2" x 1½"	"
	1½" x 6½" COPPER SHEET	

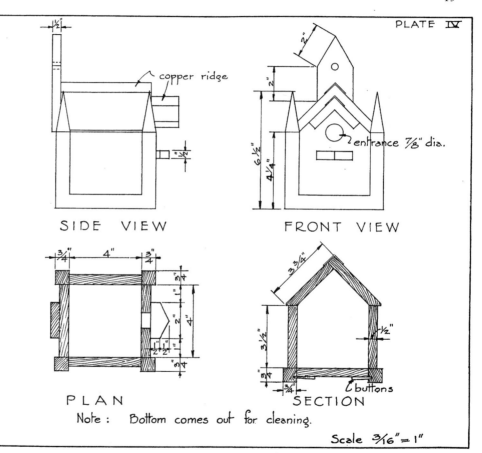

SIDE VIEW

copper ridge

FRONT VIEW

entrance ⅞" dia.

PLAN

Note: Bottom comes out for cleaning.

SECTION

buttons

Scale 3/16" = 1"

PLATE V

THE HEXAGON
WREN HOUSE

BILL OF MATERIAL

6 PC $\frac{1}{2}$" × 2$\frac{7}{8}$" × 7$\frac{1}{2}$"   SIDES

1 PC $\frac{3}{4}$" × 4$\frac{1}{2}$" HEXAGON BOTTOM

1 PC $\frac{3}{4}$" × 7"   "   TOP

1 PC $\frac{3}{4}$" × 3$\frac{1}{2}$"   "   "

1 PC $\frac{1}{4}$" × 2" ROUND   PERCH

1 1" DIAMETER RING

1     $\frac{3}{16}$" × 2" EYE BOLT

6 1" #6 FLAT HEAD SCREWS

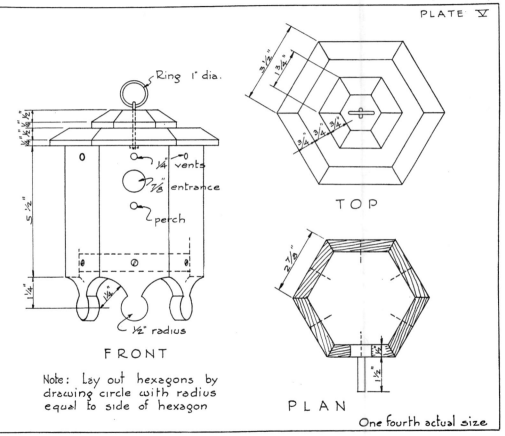

Ring 1" dia.

$\frac{1}{4}$ vents

$\frac{7}{8}$" entrance

perch

5$\frac{1}{2}$"

$\frac{1}{4}$"

$\frac{1}{2}$" radius

FRONT

Note: Lay out hexagons by
drawing circle with radius
equal to side of hexagon

3$\frac{1}{2}$"

1$\frac{3}{4}$"

$\frac{3}{4}$" $\frac{3}{4}$" $\frac{3}{4}$"

TOP

2$\frac{7}{8}$"

$\frac{1}{2}$"

$\frac{1}{2}$"

PLAN

One fourth actual size

PLATE VI.

THE DUPLEX
2 ROOM WREN HOUSE
BILL OF MATERIAL

1 PC	$3/8'' \times 4\frac{1}{2} \times 10''$	BOTTOM
2 PC	$3/8'' \times 3'' \times 3\frac{3}{4}''$	ENDS
2 PC	$3/8'' \times 7\frac{1}{2}'' \times 10''$	FRONT & BACK
2 PC	$3/8'' \times 5\frac{1}{4}'' \times 8''$	ROOF
2 PC	$3/8'' \times 3\frac{1}{2}'' \times 3\frac{1}{8}''$	DORMER ROOF
2 PC	$3/8'' \times 2'' \times 2''$	" FRONT
4 PC	$3/8'' \times 2'' \times 2''$	" SIDES
2 PC	$3/8'' \times 3\frac{3}{4}'' \times 7\frac{1}{2}''$	PARTITION
1 PC	$3/8'' \times 1\frac{1}{2}'' \times 3''$	HANGER
1 PAIR	HINGES	
1 HOOK AND EYE		

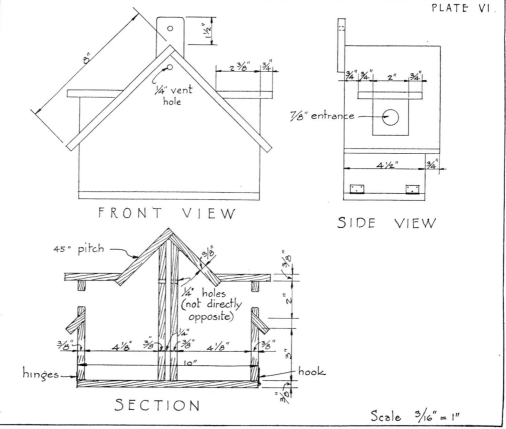

FRONT VIEW

¼" vent hole

8"

1½"

2⅜" ¾"

SIDE VIEW

7/8" entrance

¾" ¾" 2" ¾"

4½" ¾"

SECTION

45° pitch

3/8"

¼" holes (not directly opposite)

3/8" 2" 3"

hinges

3/8" 4⅛" 3/8" 3/8" 4⅛" 3/8"

10"

hook

Scale $3/16'' = 1''$

PLATE VII

THE "CLOCK"

TWO ROOM WREN HOUSE
BILL OF MATERIAL

1	PC	½" x 4" x 9½"	BOTTOM
2	PC	½" x 11½" x 9"	FRONT & BACK
2	PC	½" x 4" x 5"	SIDES
1	PC	½" x 4" x 7½"	PARTITION
2	PC	½" x 6½" x 7½"	ROOF
2	PC	¼" ROUND x 2½"	PERCH
1	PC	½" x 1" x 6"	HANGER
2		TIN CLOCK HANDS	
1		HINGE	
1		HOOK	
2		PINE CONES	
7"		SASH CHAIN	

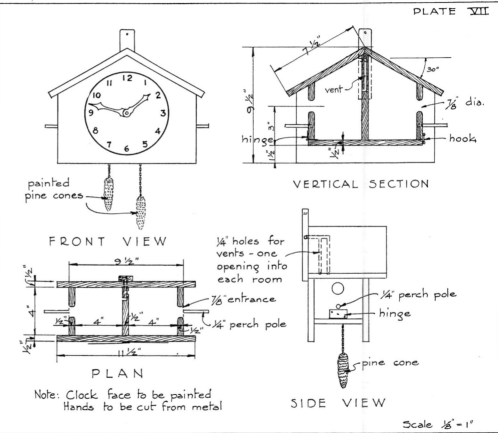

FRONT VIEW

painted pine cones

VERTICAL SECTION

vent

hinge

⅞" dia.

hook

7½"

9½"

3"

30°

PLAN

9½"

11½"

4"

4"

⅞" entrance

¼" perch pole

¼" holes for vents - one opening into each room

¼" perch pole

hinge

pine cone

SIDE VIEW

Note: Clock face to be painted
Hands to be cut from metal

Scale ⅛" = 1"

BUNGALOW
WREN HOUSE
BILL OF MATERIAL

1 PC	⅜" × 6" × 9½"		BOTTOM
1 PC	⅜" × 1⅝" × 6½"		PORCH FLOOR
1 PC	⅜" × 2⅛" × 3¼"	"	"
2 PC	⅜" × 4" × 5½"		ENDS
1 PC	⅜" × 6¼" × 4"		FRONT
1 PC	⅜" × 6¼" × 2¾"		DRAWER
1 PC	⅜" × 6¼" × 1"		BACK
1 PC	¼" × 3⅝" × 6¼"		DRAWER BOTTOM
1 PC	⅜" × 4" × 7"		FRONT PORCH ROOF
4 PC	⅜" × ⅜" × 2"	"	" POSTS
1 PC	⅜" × ¾" × 6¼"	"	" BEAM
2 PC	⅜" × ¾" × 1¼"	"	"
2 PC	⅜" × 1" × 2⅛"	SIDE	"
2 PC	⅜" × ⅜" × 1⅜"	"	" POSTS
2 PC	⅜" × ¾" × 1¾"	"	" BEAM
1 PC	⅜" × ¾" × 3¼"	"	"
2 PC	¼" × ½" × 1¾"	"	" RAIL
2 PC	¾" × 3¾" × 8½"	ROOF	
1 PC	⅜" × 3½" × 4"	DORMER ROOF	
1 PC	⅜" × 3¼" × 2¼"	"	FRONT
2 PC	⅜" × 2½" × 1¾"	"	SIDES
2 PC	¾" × 1" × 1½"	CHIMNEY	
2 PC	¼" × 1" × 1¼"	"	CAP

OYSTER SHELLS ON FRESH PAINT FOR STUCCO

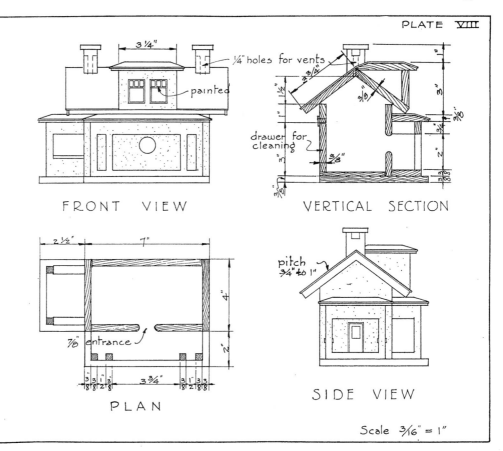

FRONT VIEW

3¼"

¼" holes for vents

painted

VERTICAL SECTION

3¾"

⅜"

drawer for cleaning

⅜"

PLAN

2½" 7"

4"

2"

⅞" entrance

3¾"

SIDE VIEW

pitch ¾" to 1"

Scale ³⁄₁₆" = 1"

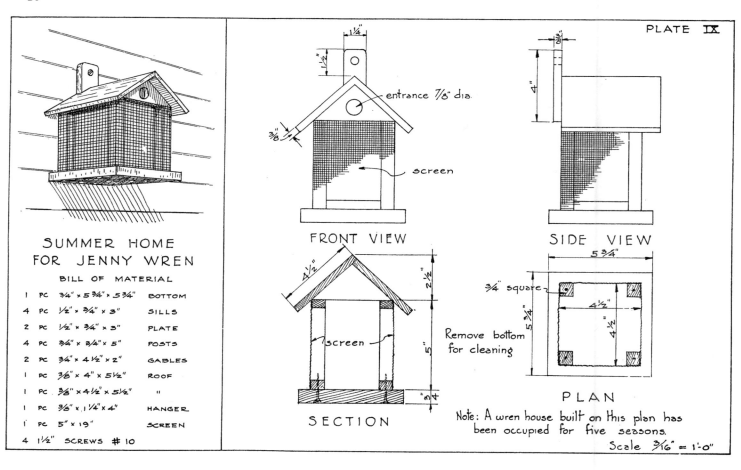

PLATE IX

SUMMER HOME FOR JENNY WREN

BILL OF MATERIAL

1	PC	3/4" x 5 3/4" x 5 3/4"	BOTTOM
4	PC	1/2" x 3/4" x 3"	SILLS
2	PC	1/2" x 3/4" x 3"	PLATE
4	PC	3/4" x 3/4" x 5"	POSTS
2	PC	3/4" x 4 1/2" x 2"	GABLES
1	PC	3/8" x 4" x 5 1/2"	ROOF
1	PC	3/8" x 4 1/2" x 5 1/2"	"
1	PC	3/8" x 1 1/4" x 4"	HANGER
1	PC	5" x 19"	SCREEN
4	1 1/2" SCREWS # 10		

entrance 7/8" dia.

screen

FRONT VIEW

SIDE VIEW

screen

3/4" square

Remove bottom for cleaning

SECTION

PLAN

Note: A wren house built on this plan has been occupied for five seasons.

Scale 3/16" = 1'-0"

PLATE X

OBSERVATION WREN HOUSE

BILL OF MATERIAL

1	PC	3/8" x 4 3/4 x 8"	BOTTOM
2	PC	3/8" x 5 3/4" x 4'	SIDES
2	PC	3/8" x 3 5/8" x 4"	ENDS
1	PC	1 1/4" x 4 3/4" x 8"	TOP
1	PC	1/4" x 3/4" x 1 1/2"	PERCH
1	PC	3 1/8" x 4'	GLASS
1	PAIR HINGES		
1	HOOK		
1	KNOB		
1	EYE		

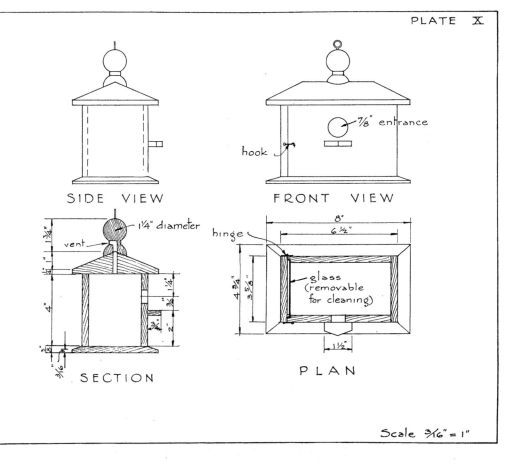

SIDE VIEW

FRONT VIEW

7/8" entrance

hook

SECTION

1 1/4" diameter

vent

PLAN

hinge

glass (removable for cleaning)

Scale 3/16" = 1"

WREN HOUSE

A wren house should have the following dimensions: Floor 4" × 4"; depth 6" to 8"; entrance should be from 1" to 6" above the floor, and the diameter ⅞". This is large enough for a wren and too small for a sparrow, which makes the wren house sparrow-proof. Most wren houses are provided with a perch, although the bird can manage without one. The perch helps the bird, especially when building, as it furnishes a landing place when putting in the nesting material. The house should be placed 6 to 10 feet above the ground. (Plates I to X.)

BLUEBIRD HOUSE

A bluebird house should have the following dimensions: Floor 5" × 5"; depth 8"; entrance should be from 2" to 6" above the floor, and the diameter 1½". A bluebird house is more practical if it has a perch, but it is not absolutely necessary. If the wood is painted it makes a smooth surface but is harder for the bird to obtain a footing. A bluebird will build in a swinging house which the English sparrow does not like, thus protecting the bluebird from these pests. The house should be placed 5 to 10 feet above the ground. (Plates XI to XVII.)

MARTIN HOUSE

The rooms in a martin house should have the following dimensions: Floor 6" × 6"; depth of room 6"; entrance 2½" in diameter. The martin is a medium-sized bird and requires a large entrance. Experience has proven that 2" is the proper distance for the entrance to be placed above the floor. An entrance placed on a level with the floor endangers the young birds which might fall out of the nest. Likewise the higher entrance prevents rain from blowing in upon the nest.

A porch from 4" to 6" wide on a martin house is a necessity. The martin enjoys a wide porch on which it can rest in the sun. Never place a railing around this porch. The house should be 15 to 20 feet from the ground.[1] (Plates XVIII to XXVb.)

(continued on page 38)

---

[1]The dimensions of the foregoing houses were taken from U.S. Department of Agriculture, Farmers' Bulletin No. 609.

The entrance to the bluebird house is given in the government bulletin as 6" above the floor, and the entrance to the martin house as 1" above the floor, but experience has proven that the dimensions given in the drawings are more practical.

THE ROUND HOUSE

BLUEBIRD HOUSE

BILL OF MATERIAL

1 7½" SECTION OF 8" PORCH COLUMN
1 PC ¾" x 8½" DIAMETER BOTTOM
1 PC ¾" x 9½"   "   TOP
1 PC ¾" x 4½"   "   "
1 PC ¼" x 3" ROUND PERCH
1 PC ¼" x 3¼"   "   "
1 KNOB
3 2" #11 SCREWS

PLATE XI

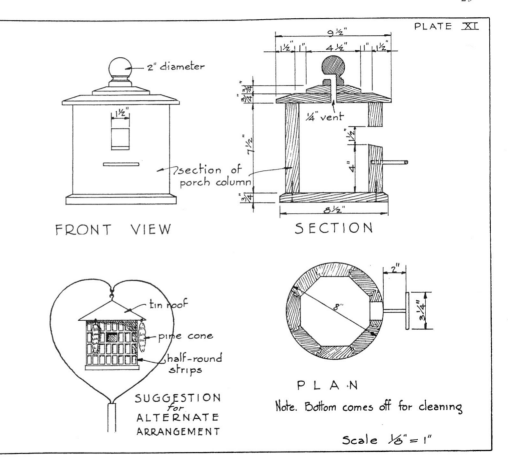

FRONT VIEW

2" diameter
1½"
?section of porch column

SECTION

9½"
1½" 1" 4½" 1" 1½"
¾"
¼" vent
7½"
½"
4"
¾"
8½"

SUGGESTION
for
ALTERNATE
ARRANGEMENT

tin roof
pine cone
half-round strips

PLAN

2"
8"
3¼"

Note. Bottom comes off for cleaning

Scale ⅛" = 1"

PLATE XII

JAPANESE LANTERN

BLUEBIRD HOUSE

BILL OF MATERIAL

6 PC	½" × 4" × 7¼"	SIDES	
1 PC	¾" × 10" HEXAGON	BOTTOM	
1 PC	¾" × 11"	"	TOP
1 PC	½" × 7"	"	"
1 PC	¾" × 3"	"	"
6 PC	¼" ROUND × 5"	HIP	
2 PC	¼" " × 2"	PERCH	
1 RING WITH SCREW EYE			

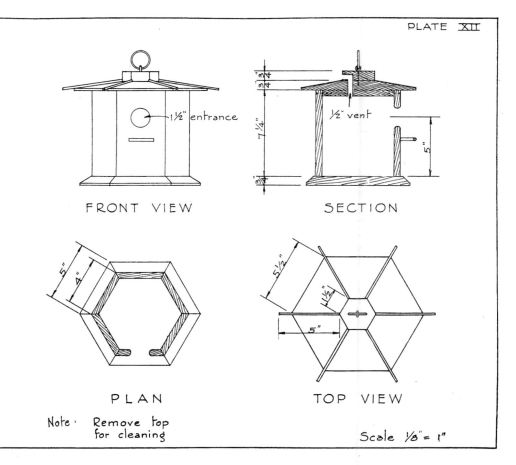

FRONT VIEW — 1½" entrance

SECTION — ½" vent — 7¼" — 5"

PLAN — 5" — 4"

TOP VIEW — 5½" — 1½" — 5"

Note: Remove top for cleaning

Scale ⅛" = 1"

PLATE XIII

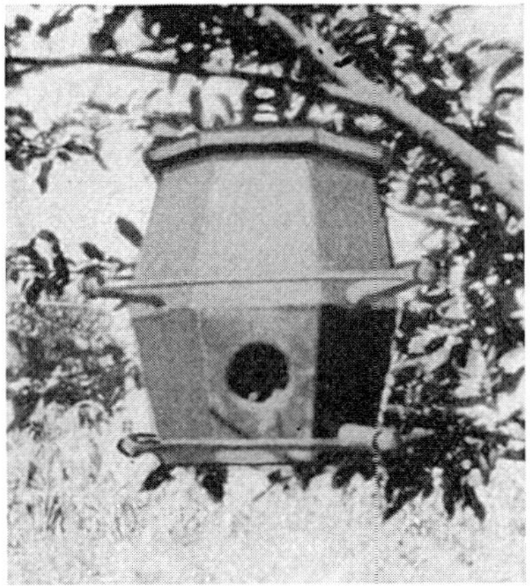

"OCTAGON"

TWO ROOM BLUEBIRD HOUSE

BILL OF MATERIAL

12	PC	¾" x 3¼" to 4" x 7½"	SIDES
1	PC	¾" x 8½" OCTAGON	BOTTOM
1	PC	¾" x 10½" "	2ND FLOOR
1	PC	¾" x 8½" "	TOP
1	PC	¾" x 5½" "	"
8	PC	¼" x 2½"	PERCH POLES
90"		WIRE	" RINGS
1		KNOB	

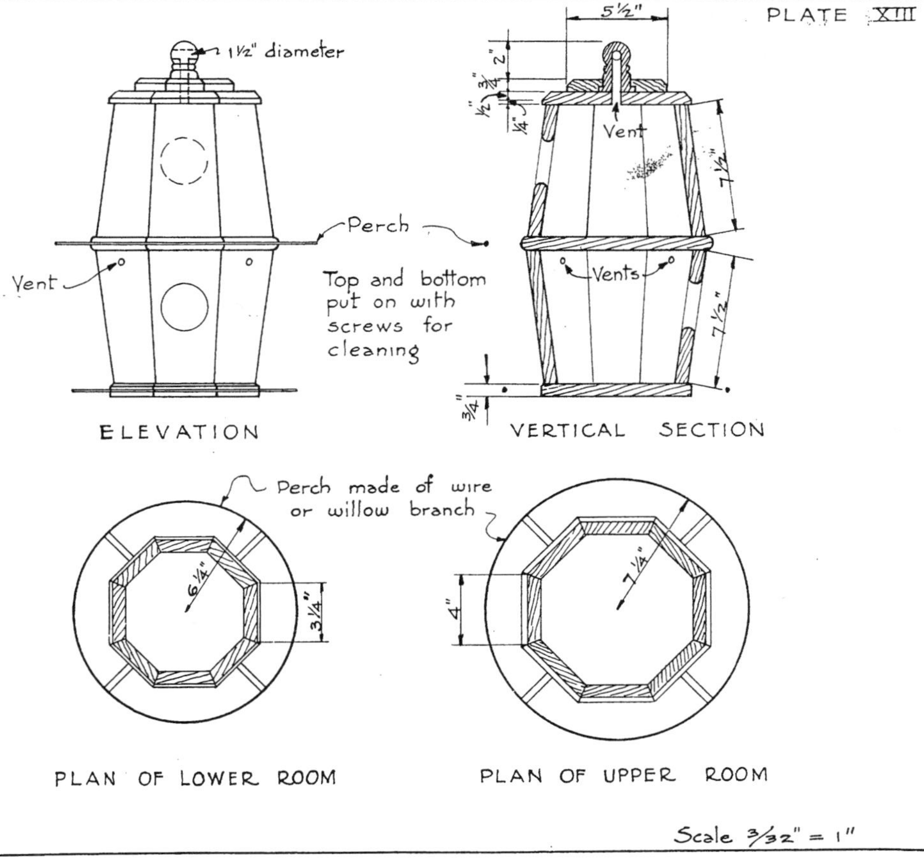

1½" diameter
Vent
Perch
Top and bottom put on with screws for cleaning
ELEVATION
5½"
7½"
7½"
Vent
Vents
VERTICAL SECTION
Perch made of wire or willow branch
6¼"
3¼"
PLAN OF LOWER ROOM
4"
7¼"
PLAN OF UPPER ROOM
Scale 3/32" = 1"

PLATE XIV

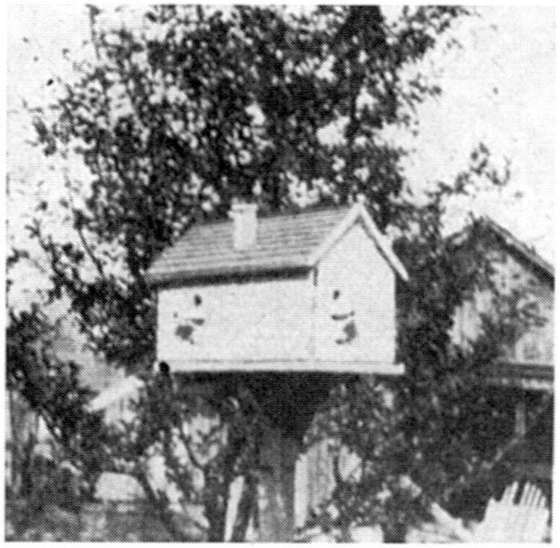

THE COTTAGE

FOUR ROOM BLUE BIRD HOUSE

BILL OF MATERIAL

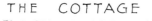

1	PC	3/4" x 18" x 18"	BOTTOM
2	PC	1/2" x 12 3/4" x 8"	SIDES
2	PC	1/2" x 13 3/4" x 12"	ENDS
1	PC	3/4" x 7 1/2" x 12 3/4"	PARTITION
2	PC	3/4" x 7 1/2" x 6"	"
1	PC	1/2" x 12 3/4" x 12 3/4"	CEILING
2	PC	1/2" x 10" x 18"	ROOF
1	PC	1" x 1 1/2" x 2 1/2"	CHIMNEY
1	PC	1/4" x 1 1/4" x 1 3/4"	" CAP
4	PC	1/2" x 1 1/2" x 2 1/2"	PERCH
4	PC	1/2" x 1 1/4" x 2 1/2"	" BR'CKETS
1	PAIR HINGES		
1	HOOK		

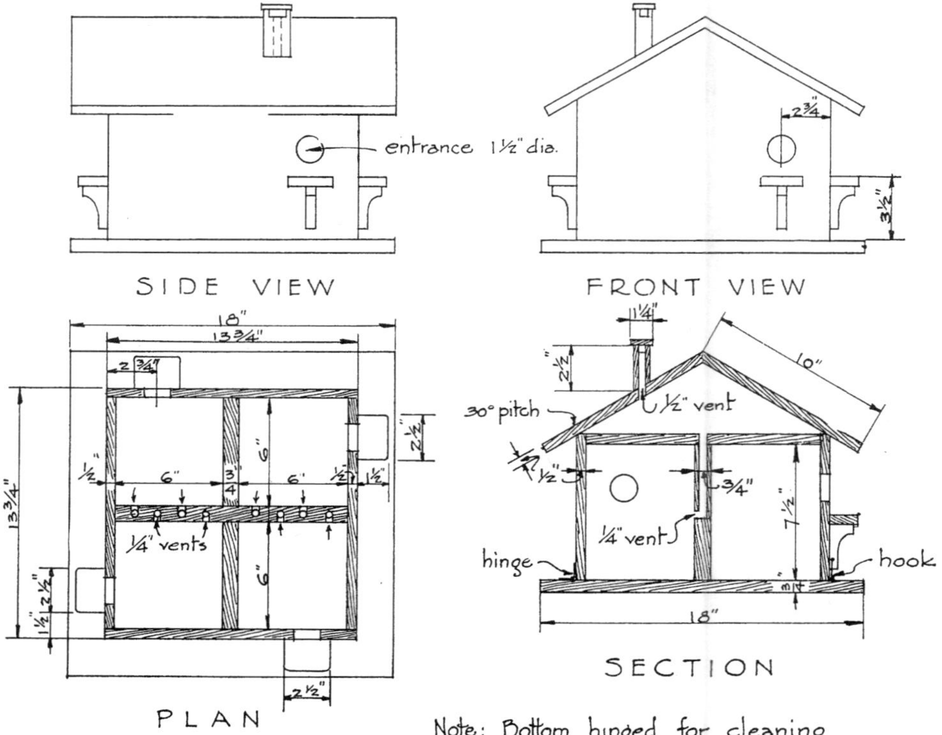

entrance 1 1/2" dia.
2 3/4"
3 1/2"
SIDE VIEW
FRONT VIEW
18"
13 3/4"
2 3/4"
2 1/2"
1/2"
6"
3/4
1 1/2"
1/4" vents
PLAN
1 1/4"
10"
30° pitch
1/2" vent
1/4" vent
7 1/2"
hinge
hook
18"
SECTION

Note: Bottom hinged for cleaning

Scale 3/32" = 1"

PLATE XV

ENGLISH COTTAGE
2 ROOM BLUEBIRD HOUSE
BILL OF MATERIAL

1 PC	3/4" x 8" x 14"	BOTTOM	
1 PC	3/4" x 1 1/2" x 4 1/4"	PORCH FLOOR	
1 PC	3/8" x 11 1/8" x 6"	BACK	
1 PC	3/8" x 11 1/8" x 7 3/4"	FRONT	
2 PC	3/8" x 6" x 6"	ENDS	
1 PC	3/8" x 6" x 10"	PARTITIONS	
2 PC	3/8" x 11 1/8" x 5 1/2"	ROOF	
2 PC	3/8" x 6" x 4 3/8"	"	
1 PC	3/8" x 1 1/2" x 3"	PORCH	
2 PC	3/8" x 3/8" x 2"	" COLUMN	
1 PC	3/4" x 1 1/2" x 3"	" ROOF	
2 PC	1/4" x 2 1/2" x 1"	PERCH	
2 PC	3/4" x 2 1/2" x 11 1/4"	CHIMNEYS	
2 PC	1/4" QUARTER RD.	PERCH	
1 PAIR HINGES			
1 HOOK			

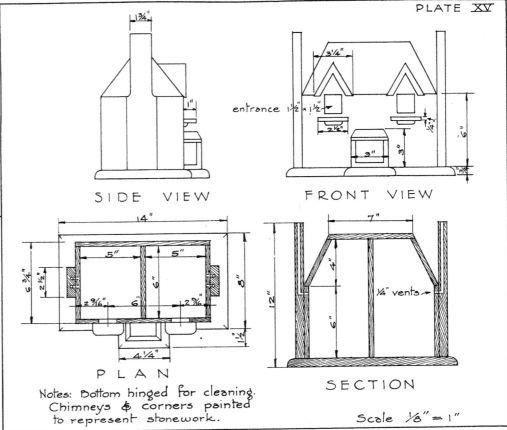

SIDE VIEW

entrance 1 1/2" x 1 1/2"

FRONT VIEW

PLAN

SECTION

Notes: Bottom hinged for cleaning.
Chimneys & corners painted
to represent stonework.

Scale 1/8" = 1"

JAPANESE BLUEBIRD

THIS HOUSE WON SECOND
PRIZE IN A BIRDHOUSE CONTEST

BILL OF MATERIAL

6 PC	$\frac{1}{2}'' \times 5''$ to $3\frac{1}{2}'' \times 9\frac{1}{2}''$	SIDES
6 PC	$\frac{1}{2}'' \times 5''$ to $2'' \times 4\frac{1}{2}''$	"
1 PC	$\frac{3}{4}'' \times 4''$ HEXAGON	TOP
1 PC	$\frac{3}{4}'' \times 2''$ "	"
1 PC	$\frac{3}{4}'' \times 7''$ "	BOTTOM
130"	$\frac{1}{4}'' \times \frac{3}{8}''$	STRIP
360"	HALF ROUND	"
1 PC	7" BENT TWIG	PERCH
1 HOOK		

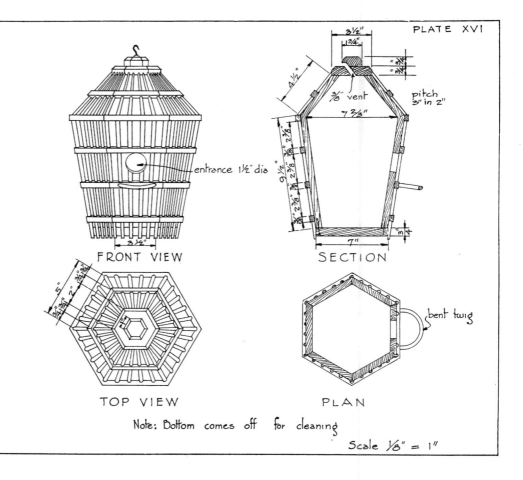

PLATE XVI

$\frac{3}{8}''$ vent

pitch 3" in 2"

entrance $1\frac{1}{2}''$ dia

FRONT VIEW   **SECTION**

bent twig

TOP VIEW   **PLAN**

Note: Bottom comes off for cleaning

Scale $\frac{1}{8}'' = 1''$

PLATE   XVII

OBSERVATION
BLUE BIRD HOUSE
BILL OF MATERIAL

1 PC	3/4" x 7" x 7"	BOTTOM
2 PC	1/2" x 6" x 8"	FRONT & BACK
2 PC	1/2" x 5" x 8"	SIDES
1 PC	3/4" x 8" x 8"	TOP
1 PC	1 1/2" x 2" x 2"	CAP
1 PC	1/4" x 1 1/2" x 2 1/4"	PERCH
1 PC	1/4" x 1 3/4"	"
2 PC	1/4" x 3 1/4" x 2 1/2"	SHUTTERS
1 PC	5 1/4" x 8"	GLASS
1 PAIR HINGES		
1 HOOK & EYE		

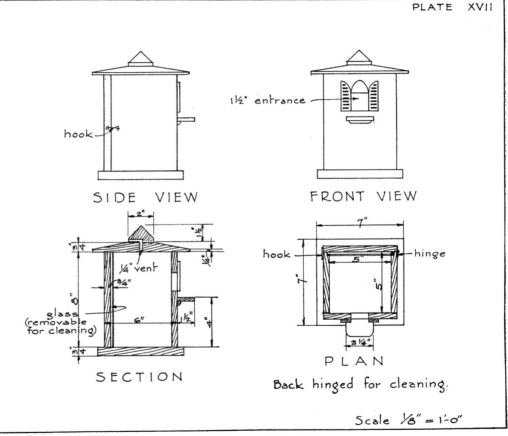

hook

SIDE VIEW

1½" entrance

FRONT VIEW

¼" vent

glass
(removable
for cleaning)

SECTION

hook   hinge

PLAN

Back hinged for cleaning.

Scale ⅛" = 1'-0"

PLATE XVIII

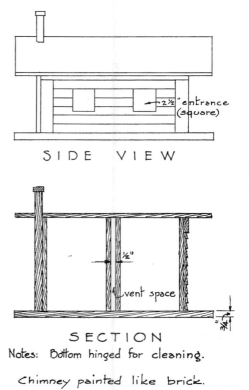

THE CABIN

4 ROOM MARTIN HOUSE
THIS HOUSE WON FIRST PRIZE
IN A BIRD HOUSE CONTEST
BILL OF MATERIAL

1 PC	3/4" x 20" x 22"	BOTTOM
2 PC	1/2" x 13 1/2" x 10 1/4"	ENDS
2 PC	1/2" x 14 1/2" x 7 1/4"	SIDES
2 PC	1/2" x 12 1/2" x 10 1/4"	PARTITIONS
2 PC	1/2" x 6 1/2" x 10 1/4"	"
2 PC	1/2" x 10 1/2" x 22"	ROOF
1 PC	3/4" x 4" x 13"	CHIMNEY
1 PC	1/2" x 1" x 3 1/4"	" CAP
4 PC	1/2" x 1" x 6"	CORNER BOARD
4 PC	1/2" x 1 1/2" x 6"	"
62"	1/2" x 1 1/2"	FRIEZE
220"	1/2" x 1"	BEVEL SIDING

END VIEW

SIDE VIEW

2 1/2" entrance (square)

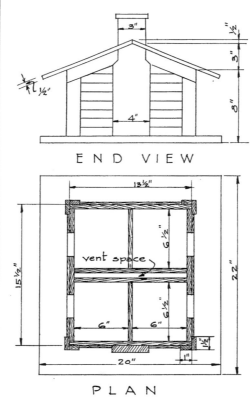

vent space

PLAN

SECTION

Notes: Bottom hinged for cleaning.

Chimney painted like brick.

Scale 3/32" = 1"

PLATE XIX

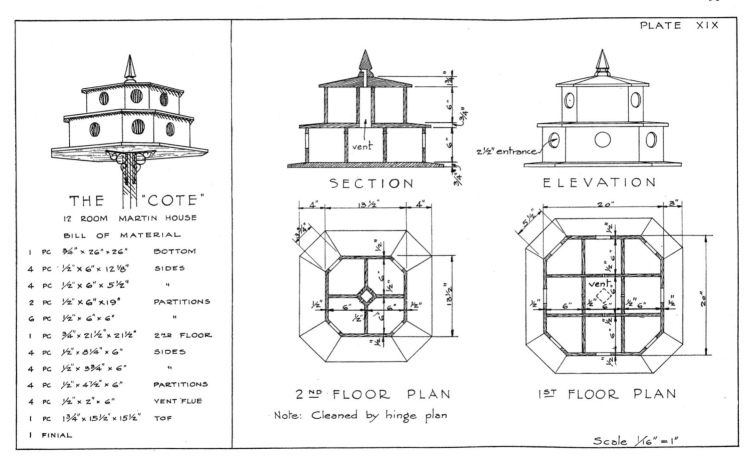

THE "COTE"

12 ROOM MARTIN HOUSE

BILL OF MATERIAL

1	PC	¾" × 26" × 26"	BOTTOM
4	PC	½" × 6" × 12⅛"	SIDES
4	PC	½" × 6" × 5½"	"
2	PC	½" × 6" × 19"	PARTITIONS
6	PC	½" × 6" × 6"	"
1	PC	¾" × 21½" × 21½"	2ND FLOOR
4	PC	½" × 8¼" × 6"	SIDES
4	PC	½" × 3¾" × 6"	"
4	PC	½" × 4½" × 6"	PARTITIONS
4	PC	½" × 2" × 6"	VENT FLUE
1	PC	1¾" × 15½" × 15½"	TOF
1	FINIAL		

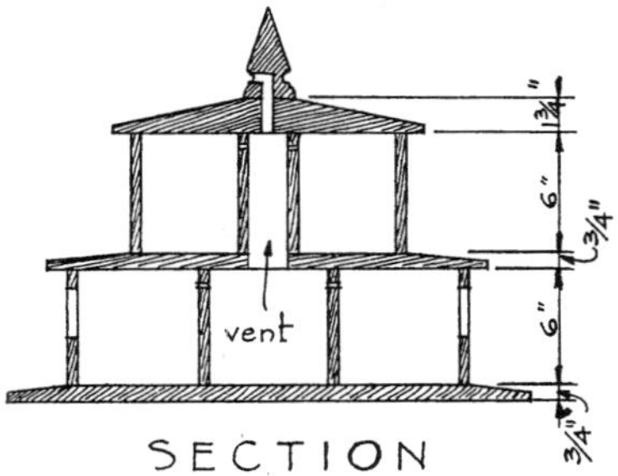

SECTION

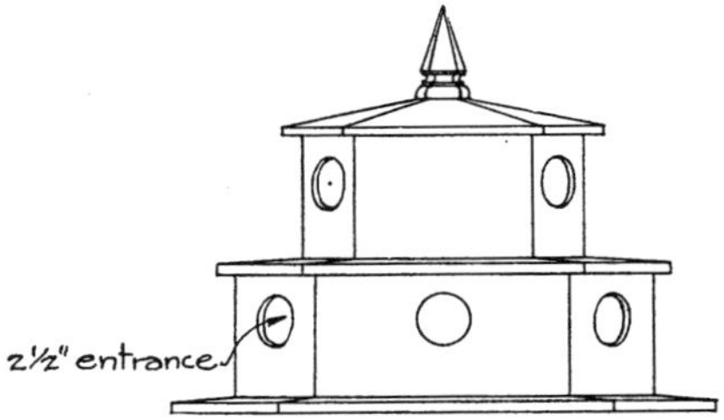

ELEVATION

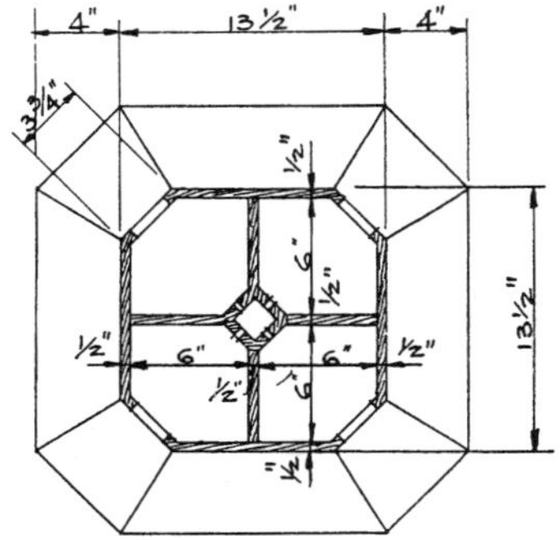

2ND FLOOR PLAN

Note: Cleaned by hinge plan

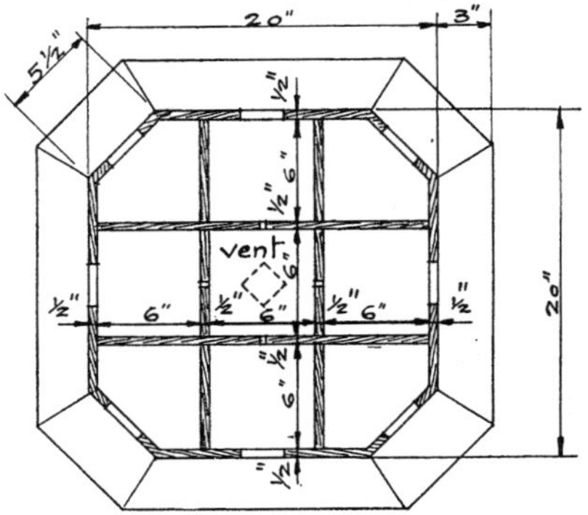

1ST FLOOR PLAN

Scale 1/16" = 1"

32

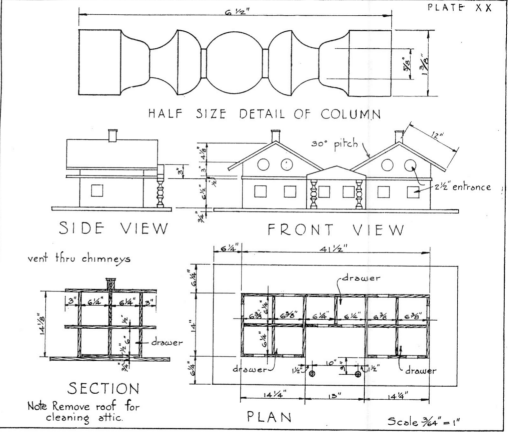

PLATE XX

HALF SIZE DETAIL OF COLUMN

SIDE VIEW   FRONT VIEW

30° pitch

2½" entrance

vent thru chimneys

SECTION
Note Remove roof for
cleaning attic.

PLAN

Scale ³⁄₆₄" = 1"

drawer

THE PLAZA
18 ROOM MARTIN HOUSE
BILL OF MATERIAL

1	PC	¾" × 26½" × 54"	BOTTOM
2	PC	½" × 6½" × 14"	SIDES
2	PC	½" × 6½" × 13½"	"
2	PC	½" × 6½" × 13"	"
2	PC	½" × 6½" × 13¼"	"
2	PC	½" × 13¼" × 13"	DRAWER BOTTOM
1	PC	½" × 6¼" × 13"	"
2	PC	½" × 6" × 13¼"	PARTITIONS
5	PC	½" × 6" × 6½"	"
1	PC	½" × 20" × 42"	2ND FLOOR
2	PC	½" × 3" × 14"	SIDES
4	PC	½" × 7" × 18"	"
2	PC	½" × 12" × 20"	ROOF
2	PC	½" × 16" × 20"	"
2	PC	½" × 7" × 16"	PARTITIONS
2	PC	½" × 6" × 6¼"	"
2	PC	1½" × 1½" × 3"	CHIMNEY
1	PC	1½" × 3" × 13"	PORCH
2		6½"	COLUMNS

THE COLONIAL

11-ROOM MARTIN HOUSE

BILL OF MATERIAL

1	PC	3/4" x 18" x 22"	BOTTOM
2	PC	1/2" x 18" x 22"	FLOORS
4	PC	1/2" x 13 1/2" x 6"	SIDES
4	PC	1/2" x 8 1/2" x 6"	ENDS
2	PC	1/2" x 12 1/2" x 6"	PARTITIONS
2	PC	1/2" x 4" x 6"	"
2	PC	1/2" x 22" x 11"	ROOF
4	PC	1/2" x 15" x 6 1/2"	ATTIC PARTITIONS
1	PC	1/2" x 4" x 4"	DORMER FRONT
2	PC	1/2" x 4" x 4"	" SIDES
2	PC	1 1/2" x 2" x 3"	CHIMNEY
2	PC	1/4" x 1 3/4" x 2 1/4"	" CAP
16		6"	COLUMNS

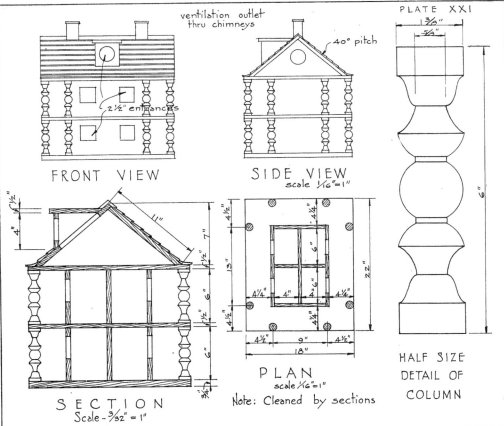

ventilation outlet
thru chimneys

2 1/2" entrances

FRONT VIEW

40° pitch

SIDE VIEW
scale 1/16"=1"

11"

2 1/2"

4"

7"

1 1/2"

6"

1 1/2"

6"

3/4"

SECTION
Scale - 3/32" = 1"

4 1/2"

4 1/4"

13"

6"

6"

22"

4 1/2"

4 1/4"

4"

4 1/2"

4 1/4"

4 1/2"

9"

4 1/2"

18"

PLAN
scale 1/16"=1"

Note: Cleaned by sections

PLATE XXI

1 3/8"

5/8"

6"

HALF SIZE
DETAIL OF
COLUMN

PLATE XXII

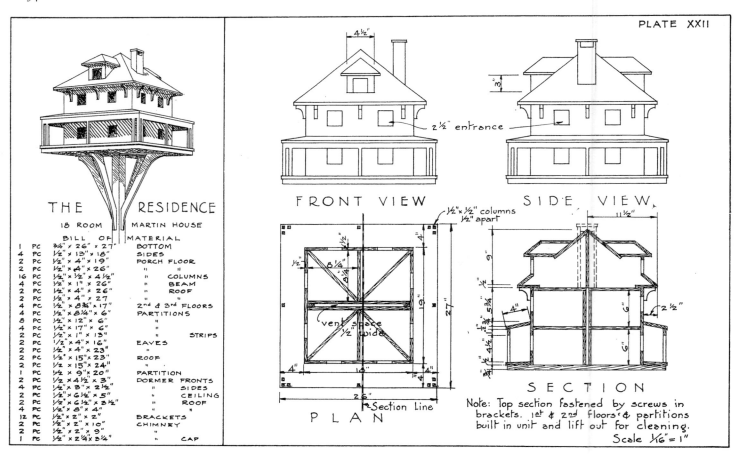

THE RESIDENCE

18 ROOM MARTIN HOUSE

BILL OF MATERIAL

1 PC	$\frac{3}{4}$" x 26" x 27"	BOTTOM	
4 PC	$\frac{1}{2}$" x 13" x 18"	SIDES	
2 PC	$\frac{1}{2}$" x 4" x 19"	PORCH FLOOR	
2 PC	$\frac{1}{2}$" x 4" x 26"	"	
16 PC	$\frac{1}{2}$" x $\frac{1}{2}$" x 4 $\frac{1}{2}$"	" COLUMNS	
4 PC	$\frac{1}{2}$" x 1" x 26"	" BEAM	
2 PC	$\frac{1}{2}$" x 4" x 26"	" ROOF	
2 PC	$\frac{1}{2}$" x 4" x 27"		
4 PC	$\frac{1}{2}$" x 8 $\frac{3}{4}$" x 17"	2nd & 3rd FLOORS	
4 PC	$\frac{1}{2}$" x 8 $\frac{1}{4}$" x 6"	PARTITIONS	
8 PC	$\frac{1}{2}$" x 12" x 6"		
4 PC	$\frac{1}{2}$" x 17" x 6"		
2 PC	$\frac{1}{2}$" x 1" x 13"	STRIPS	
2 PC	$\frac{1}{2}$" x 4" x 16"	EAVES	
2 PC	$\frac{1}{2}$" x 4" x 23"	"	
2 PC	$\frac{1}{2}$" x 15" x 23"	ROOF	
2 PC	$\frac{1}{2}$ x 15" x 24"	"	
1 PC	$\frac{1}{2}$" x 9" x 20"	PARTITION	
2 PC	$\frac{1}{2}$" x 4 $\frac{1}{2}$" x 3"	DORMER FRONTS	
4 PC	$\frac{1}{2}$" x 8" x 2 $\frac{1}{2}$"	" SIDES	
2 PC	$\frac{1}{2}$" x 6 $\frac{1}{2}$" x 5"	" CEILING	
2 PC	$\frac{1}{2}$" x 6 $\frac{1}{2}$" x 3 $\frac{1}{2}$"	" ROOF	
4 PC	$\frac{1}{2}$" x 8" x 4"		
12 PC	$\frac{1}{2}$" x 2" x 2"	BRACKETS	
2 PC	$\frac{1}{2}$" x 2" x 10"	CHIMNEY	
2 PC	$\frac{1}{2}$" x 2" x 9"	"	
1 PC	$\frac{1}{2}$" x 2 $\frac{1}{4}$" x 3 $\frac{3}{4}$"	" CAP	

FRONT VIEW

SIDE VIEW

2 $\frac{1}{2}$" entrance

PLAN

Section Line

SECTION

Note: Top section fastened by screws in brackets. 1st & 2nd floors & partitions built in unit and lift out for cleaning.

Scale $\frac{1}{16}$" = 1"

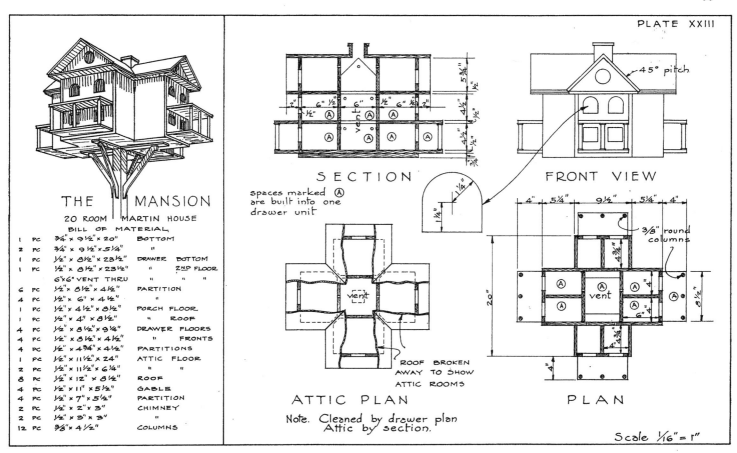

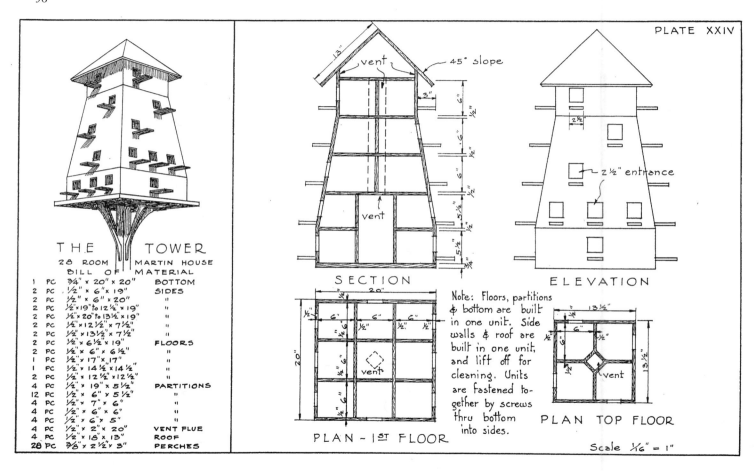

PLATE XXIV

THE TOWER
28 ROOM MARTIN HOUSE
BILL OF MATERIAL

1 PC	3/4" x 20" x 20"	BOTTOM	
2 PC	1/2" x 6" x 19"	SIDES	
2 PC	1/2" x 6" x 20"	"	
2 PC	1/2" x 19" to 12 1/2" x 19"	"	
2 PC	1/2" x 20" to 13 1/2" x 19"	"	
2 PC	1/2" x 12 1/2" x 7 1/2"	"	
2 PC	1/2" x 13 1/2" x 7 1/2"	"	
2 PC	1/2" x 6 1/2" x 19"	FLOORS	
2 PC	1/2" x 6" x 6 1/2"	"	
1 PC	1/2" x 17" x 17"	"	
1 PC	1/2" x 14 1/2" x 14 1/2"	"	
2 PC	1/2" x 12 1/2" x 12 1/2"	"	
4 PC	1/2" x 19" x 5 1/2"	PARTITIONS	
12 PC	1/2" x 6" x 5 1/2"	"	
4 PC	1/2" x 7" x 6"	"	
4 PC	1/2" x 6" x 6"	"	
4 PC	1/2" x 6" x 5"	"	
4 PC	1/2" x 2" x 20"	VENT FLUE	
4 PC	1/2" x 18" x 13"	ROOF	
28 PC	3/8" x 2 1/2" x 3"	PERCHES	

vent

45° slope

13"

3"

6"

1/2"

6"

1/2"

6"

1/2"

5 1/2"

1/2"

5 1/2"

3/4"

vent

SECTION

ELEVATION

2 1/2"

2 1/2" entrance

Note: Floors, partitions
& bottom are built
in one unit. Side
walls & roof are
built in one unit,
and lift off for
cleaning. Units
are fastened to-
gether by screws
thru bottom
into sides.

20"

1/2"

1/2"

6"

6"

6"

1/2"

1/2"

20"

6"

1/2"

6"

vent

6"

PLAN - 1ST FLOOR

13 1/2"

6"

1/2"

13 1/2"

1/2"

vent

PLAN TOP FLOOR

Scale 1/6" = 1"

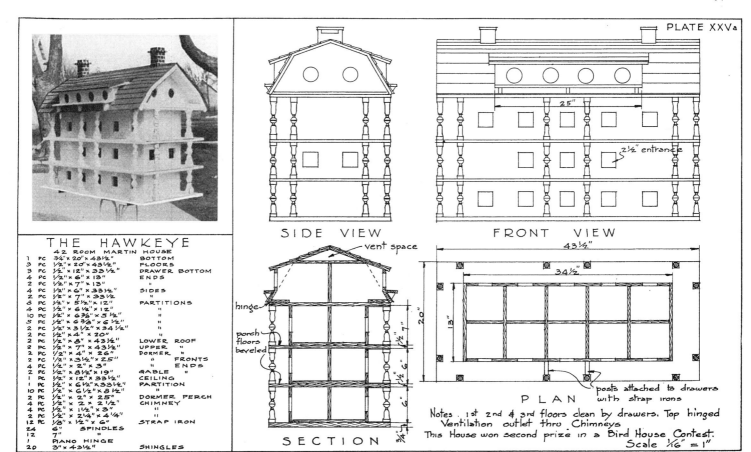

PLATE XXVa

THE HAWKEYE

42 ROOM MARTIN HOUSE

1	PC	3/4" x 20" x 43½"	BOTTOM
3	PC	½" x 20" x 43½"	FLOORS
3	PC	½" x 12" x 33½"	DRAWER BOTTOM
4	PC	½" x 6" x 13"	ENDS
2	PC	½" x 7" x 13"	"
4	PC	½" x 6" x 33½"	SIDES
2	PC	½" x 7" x 33½	"
8	PC	½" x 5½" x 12"	PARTITIONS
4	PC	½" x 6½" x 12"	"
10	PC	½" x 6⅜" x 5½"	"
5	PC	½" x 6⅜" x 6½"	"
2	PC	½" x 3½" x 34½"	"
2	PC	½" x 4" x 20"	"
2	PC	½" x 8" x 43½"	LOWER ROOF
2	PC	½" x 7" x 43½"	UPPER "
2	PC	½" x 4" x 26"	DORMER "
2	PC	½" x 3½" x 25"	" FRONTS
4	PC	½" x 2" x 3"	" ENDS
2	PC	½" x 8½" x 19"	GABLE "
1	PC	½" x 12" x 33½"	CEILING
1	PC	½" x 6½" x 33½"	PARTITION
10	PC	½" x 6½" x 8½"	"
2	PC	½" x 2" x 25"	DORMER PERCH
4	PC	½" x 2 x 2½"	CHIMNEY
4	PC	½" x 1½" x 3"	"
2	PC	½" x 2¼" x 4¼"	"
12	PC	1/8" x ½" x 6"	STRAP IRON
24		6" SPINDLES	
12		7" "	
1		PIANO HINGE	
20		3" x 43½"	SHINGLES

SIDE VIEW

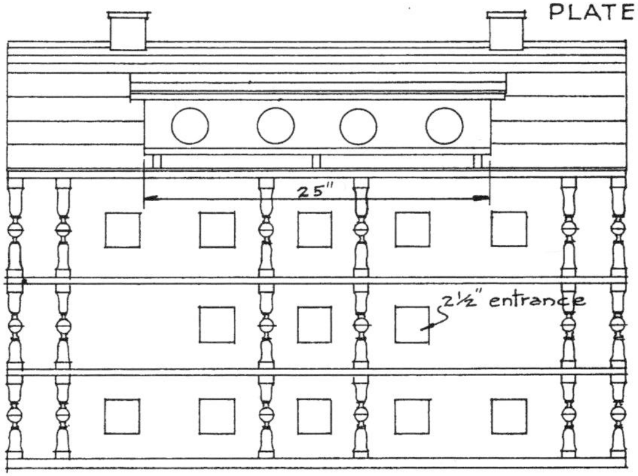
25"
2½" entrance

FRONT VIEW

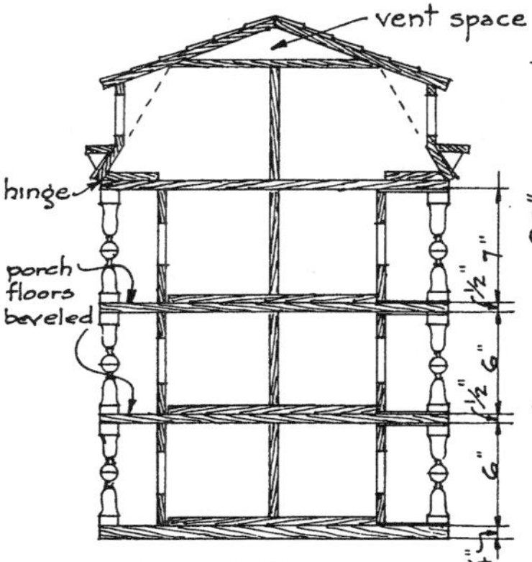
vent space
hinge
porch floors beveled
20"
7"
1½"
6"
1½"
6"
3/4"

SECTION

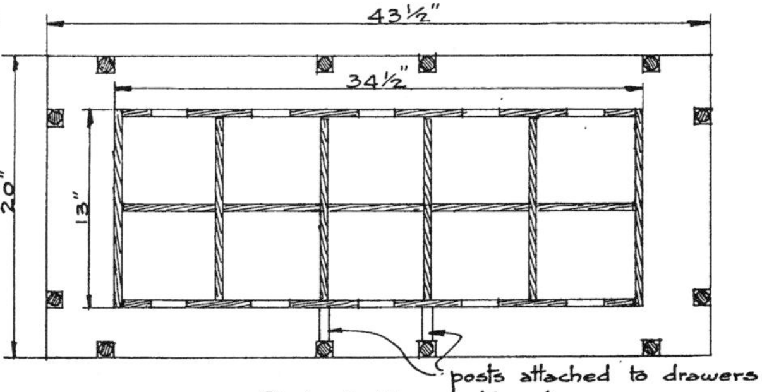
43½"
34½"
13"
posts attached to drawers with strap irons

PLAN

Notes. 1st 2nd & 3rd floors clean by drawers. Top hinged
Ventilation outlet thru Chimneys
This House won second prize in a Bird House Contest.
Scale 1/16" = 1"

VENTILATION

A birdhouse should be ventilated as it makes the house more healthful. In a small house with one room, ventilation can be furnished by boring a few holes in the sides of the house under the eaves. Never have a ventilating hole lower than the entrance.

In a large house of two or more rooms, the partition can be constructed with an air chamber between the inside walls. An air outlet should be made in the gable. If the house has a chimney, air can pass through a hole bored in its side. A large martin house with several rooms may be ventilated in the following manner. The inside walls should be constructed of ¾" material with at least five holes ⅜" in diameter bored through each inside wall, through the partition. The upper story should have holes bored in the same place making the holes continuous in the inside walls. This would provide an air chamber between each room. Holes should be bored in the side of the wall five inches from the floor, and should meet the ones bored perpendicularly in the walls. The air will be carried to the top of the room and taken up through the wall to the top of the house to the outlet. Every floor can thus be ventilated. Boring holes is much easier than making a partition between each wall. A house properly ventilated is cooler than one with no ventilation.

In summer the inside of many houses gets so warm that the young birds die from the heat. A birdhouse placed in the shade would be more healthful and cooler than one placed in the sun.

Some types of houses cannot well be placed in the shade. The martin house, for instance, should be situated in the open, away from trees, as this location is more suitable to the sailing habits of the birds. A large martin house, sheltering eight pairs of birds, needs ventilation. Sixteen parent birds, not considering the young, would foul the air in the rooms, consequently we recommend ventilation to keep the house healthful and make it cooler during the hot summer days.

OBSERVATION HOUSES FOR NATURE STUDENTS

An observation house is constructed to enable the naturalist to watch the development of eggs and young birds. Very valuable data can be gathered in this way. The house has a door on hinges. When this is opened the nest and its contents are visible through the plate

(continued on page 40)

PLATE XXV b

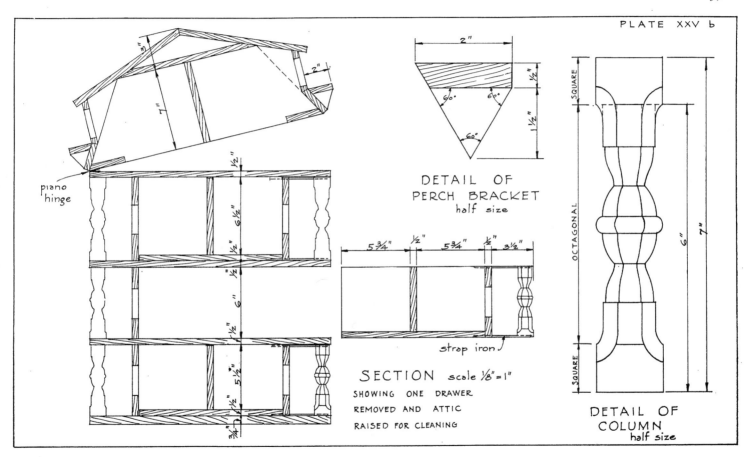

piano hinge

DETAIL OF
PERCH BRACKET
half size

SECTION scale ⅛"=1"
SHOWING ONE DRAWER
REMOVED AND ATTIC
RAISED FOR CLEANING

strop iron

DETAIL OF
COLUMN
half size

SQUARE

OCTAGONAL

SQUARE

of glass which now acts as a side to the house. Plates X and XVII show designs for observation houses.

NATURAL WOOD BOXES

Fig. 1 gives a good idea of possibilities in the use of hollow limbs, and snags in general, in building effective birdhouses.

After every windstorm, numbers of hollow limbs are found about the lawns and streets. These may be sawed into proper lengths. Well towards the top, a hole should be chiseled and then filed smooth. Next, the stump should be set on paper, and reaching through the top cavity with a pencil, an outline of the lower interior of the cavity should be sketched. With a scroll a perfect plug to fit this lower end can be cut out of half inch lumber. The exterior outline can then be drawn, and after nailing the plug to this thicker wooden base, the two will fit the bottom of the log perfectly and should be nailed there. A similar operation will complete the top. The houses can be topped with roofing material over the wooden plug.

As illustrated in No. 2, snags can easily be fit over a four or six-sided box. Nos. 4 and 5 are snags which are ready for such placement. The large snag should be placed in a box similar but larger than the second box in the illustration. Screech owls would probably take possession.

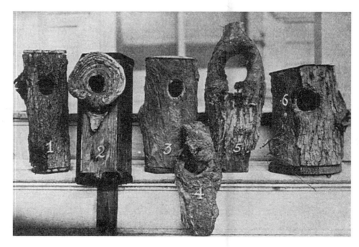

FIG. 1—NATURAL WOOD BOXES

Box No. 1, at the left, harbored black-capped chick-adees and bluebirds for three years while it was four feet from the ground. Upon placing it twelve feet up, it became the home of tufted titmice. No. 2, when placed on top of a clothesline post, captured house wrens and bluebirds. No. 3 harbored bluebirds and wrens while located on a pole, but later, when placed ten feet up on the side of a chestnut tree, it attracted red-headed woodpeckers. No. 6 was the home of great-crested flycatchers for four years.

MARTIN HOUSE

The martin house, shown in Fig. 2, has given forty years of service, and is good for several years more. When building a birdhouse one should have permanency in mind, so that the box will last for at least forty years. It can be done by following these instructions, and the finished product will be well worth the time and trouble.

Think of the great benefit the generations of martins have derived from this old house. The builder himself had no idea of the good he was rendering. The birds have returned year after year to raise their broods and in the period of forty years hundreds of martins

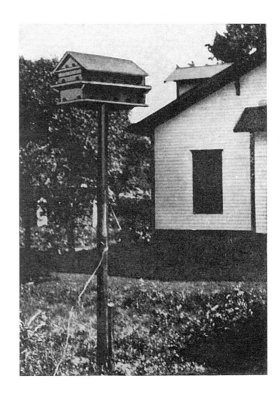

FIG. 2—MARTIN HOUSE WHICH HAS GIVEN FORTY YEARS OF SERVICE

have been reared in this house. They have returned each year and any vacant room was quickly filled by young birds who had followed their parents. A great many changes took place during that long time. The bird home builder is gone, others have come to enjoy the presence of the martins which live in the old house which has stood the storms of forty winters and summers.

During these many years the people of the community have been greatly benefited by the erection of this house. The birds, during this time, have destroyed countless millions of insects, and have been a source of pleasure because of their circling flight and warbling song.

The builder of this house deserves recognition as he has been of service to humanity, not only from an economic standpoint, but from the aesthetic as well. Others, realizing the value of the martins and the pleasure from having the birds, have followed the worthy example of the builder and have constructed similar houses. The house has twenty-eight rooms, and is large enough to accommodate fifty-six birds. It is attached to an old worm-eaten pole which shows it has stood the test of time. It is a living monument to the man who made it, and stands as a far better monument than a marble slab.

A school yard, whether a town or country school, would be an appropriate place for the location of a martin house, as the presence of the birds would be of interest to the children, teaching them to love and respect wildlife. A college campus with several martin houses properly placed about the premises would look more beautiful.

People in large cities rarely see many birds. As martins readily adapt themselves to city conditions, the people would become acquainted with them if martin houses were placed in city parks. What could be more fitting in a cemetery than several martin houses, where the birds would fill the quietness of the place with their sweet music? Birds and flowers make a good combination. A martin house located near a hospital is always of great interest to the patients. It would help them pass the many weary hours and keep their minds from their own troubles. *(continued on page 44)*

CLEANING PLANS

PLATE XXVI

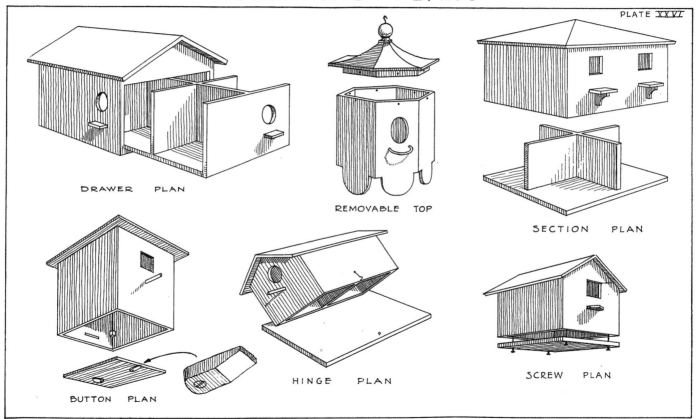

DRAWER PLAN

REMOVABLE TOP

SECTION PLAN

BUTTON PLAN

HINGE PLAN

SCREW PLAN

Each farm should have one or more martin houses to help protect the crops from insects. In the South, the natives place tall poles with cross bars, from which hang gourds. Martins nest in these, and the natives say they keep marauding hawks from the plantations.

The martins are gregarious and a large number will live under one roof. If you erect an apartment house you should soon have a colony of them. After becoming acquainted with the birds and having them on the premises, you will rejoice at their return in the spring and regret their departure in the fall.

Yearly, most states set aside a day in the spring, called Arbor and Bird Day. Trees are set out on that day, as it is dedicated to that cause and also the study of birds. Each state should not only recommend the planting of trees on that day, but should encourage the erection of birdhouses as well.

The food of the swallow is one hundred percent insect life, consisting of mosquitoes, small beetles, gnats, flies, etc., the greater part of which is taken while the bird is flying. However, some have been known to alight on the outer branches of trees and shrubs, and eat larva which infest these plants.

"A colony of sixteen pairs of martins was observed by Otto Widmann of Old Orchard, Missouri. The observation was made from 4 A.M. to 8 P.M. During this time, the parents visited their offsprings 3,277 times, averaging 205 times per pair."

At that rate, the ten pairs of birds, which, for forty years, have lived in this house, have fed a brood of four or five young birds for a ten days' period, yearly.

Each brood of four or five birds then would destroy during ten days, at least 2,050 insects. But, as the parent birds often bring several insects at one feeding, it is almost beyond the power of computation to figure the true number of the billions of insects destroyed during the forty years by the hundreds of birds born and raised in this old martin box.

CLEANING OF BIRDHOUSES

The proper time to clean out a birdhouse is in the spring before the birds return from the South. Each house should be so constructed that it can easily be cleaned. (See Fig. 3 and Plate XXVI.) All litter should be entirely removed, for some birds will not build in a house until it is cleaned of the last year's rubbish. If possible, the house should be so arranged that the sun can shine on the inside while cleaning. The sun is nature's disinfectant and will make the house more

FIG. 3—CLEANING ARRANGEMENTS
OF FORTY-TWO ROOM MARTIN HOUSE

healthful. Another advantage of an easy cleaning arrangement is that if the English sparrows start to build, the material they deposit can easily be removed.

DRAWER PLAN

The drawer plan is one of the simplest plans for cleaning of a birdhouse. The box is built like a drawer with a bottom and front. This drawer does not need a back or sides as the nesting material will stick to the bottom of the drawer. Should a sparrow build in a martin house of this plan, its rubbish can easily be removed as a drawer can be pulled out a short distance making it possible to see the sparrow's nest. Clean out the nest and push the drawer back in place.

It is a difficult task to clean out the average house situated on a high pole, and the nesting material must be pulled through an entrance which is 2½" in diameter. By the drawer plan, each drawer can be removed and emptied with ease. Each can be scrubbed on the inside, if necessary, and left in the sun to dry.

HINGE PLAN

This is a simple and easy way to clean out a birdhouse. One end of the house is hinged to the floor, and the other end is held in place by a hook. A screen door hook is preferable. When the house needs cleaning, the hook is loosened and the house leaned back, allowing space enough to remove old nesting material. This debris can be brushed into a bucket which saves littering the ground. The house can be tilted back until the sun dries the interior. The hinge plan may be applied to any kind of house, large or small. A two-story martin house can also be cleaned in this fashion. The floors should be separated by a platform and each floor cleaned separately. On large houses, strong hinges are necessary.

QUICK DETACHABLE PLAN

The detachable bottom plan is for use on small houses, such as those built for wrens or bluebirds. It would not be advisable to use this method on a large house. This principle should be used on a one-room house. When cleaning, expose the bottom and the interior to the sun.

SECTION PLAN

In the section plan, the house is made in one section. The sides of the house are screwed to the floor.

By removing the screws, the house lifts up and the partitions can be cleaned. The tower martin house is cleaned in this way. (Plate XXIV.)

OTHER CLEANING PLANS

The house can be constructed with removable top. The top is held in place by screws and the house can be cleaned by removing the screws. A similar plan is the removable bottom plan. The bottom is held on with screws.

In the door plan, the front of the box is hinged like a door and is held in place by a hook. The front of some houses are held in place with screws. These methods of cleaning are better if used on small houses.

The colonial martin house, Plate XXI, and the residence, Plate XXII, are cleaned in this way. The top story is removable. The partitions are built in one unit and lift out for cleaning. They are made similar to the partitions in an egg case. *(continued on page 48)*

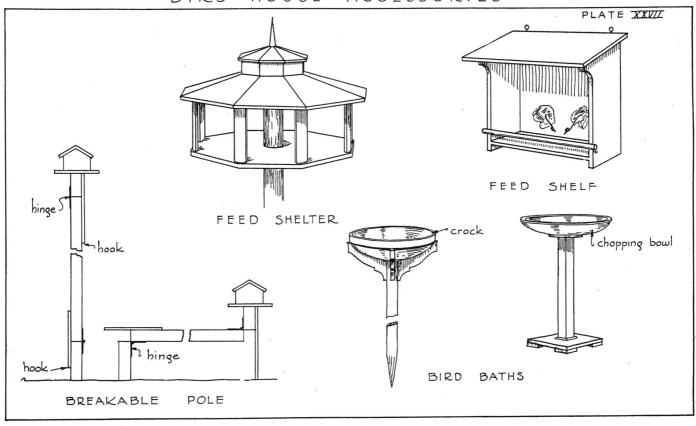

BIRD HOUSE ACCESSORIES

PLATE XXVII

FEED SHELTER

FEED SHELF

hinge

hook

hook

hinge

crock

chopping bowl

BIRD BATHS

BREAKABLE POLE

BREAKABLE POLE FOR BIRDHOUSES

A plan for this pole is shown on Plate XXVII. A pole of this type will simplify the cleaning of the house, and adapts itself particularly to martin and bluebird houses.

This type of support has a number of advantages. A pole broken only in one place makes cleaning somewhat difficult, because the sides and end of the house are parallel to the ground. Having the house upright and upon one's own level makes cleaning easy. Likewise, should the house need painting or repairing, it is more easily accomplished on the ground than when working on a ladder, which is dangerous and difficult. A house, placed on a pole of this kind, can be put up quickly and with a small amount of labor by one person. If desirable to remove the house at the close of the season, it can be done in a short time without the aid of a ladder. Another difficulty that is remedied is the problem of occupancy by the English sparrow. This bird sometimes takes possession of a martin house before that bird's return. However, a martin house on such a pole allows the owner to cover the entrance holes with cardboard. Upon the arrival of the martins in the spring, the entrance covers may be removed, and the house is ready for occupancy. This operation requires only a few minutes. Should English sparrows become established, their nests can very quickly be removed. Suggestions for entrance covers for martin houses are shown on Plate XXX.

FIG. 4—FEED SHELTER

AEROPLANE FEEDING SHELTER

This type of feeder is very popular with the winter birds. (Plate XXVIII.) *(continued on page 52)*

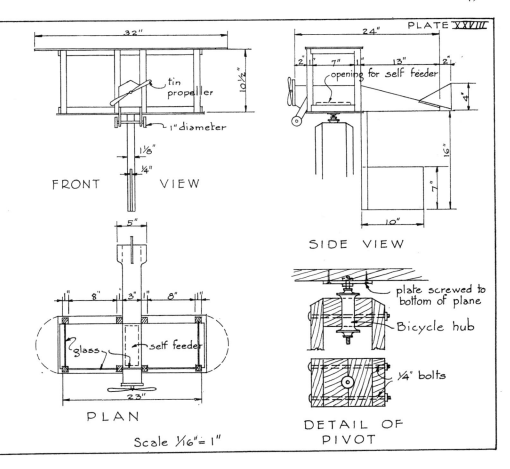

PLATE XXVIII

32"

10½"

tin
propeller

1" diameter

1⅛"

¼"

FRONT   VIEW

5"

8"   3"   8"

glass

self feeder

23"

PLAN

Scale 1/16"= 1"

24"

2"   1"   7"   1"   13"   2"

opening for self feeder

4"

16"

7"

10"

SIDE VIEW

plate screwed to
bottom of plane

Bicycle hub

¼" bolts

DETAIL OF
PIVOT

AEROPLANE FEEDING-SHELTER

2	PC	1" x 7⅜" x 24"	WINGS
8	PC	1" x 1" x 10½"	STRUTS
1	PC.	¼" x 9½" x 24½"	LOWER WING
1	PC	¼" x 9½" x 32	UPPER "
2	PC	½" x 4" x 24"	FUSELAGE SIDES
1	PC	½" x 2" x 13"	" BOTTOM
1	PC	½" x 5 & 5½" x 13"	" TOP
1	PC	½" x 4" x 5"	RUDDER
1	PC	½" x 3" x 2½"	MOTOR COVER
1	PC	½" x 3" x 7⅜"	SELF FEEDER COVER
1	PC	½" x 3½" x 4½"	FRONT
2	PC	¼" x 1" x 4½"	FORKS
1	PC	¼" ROUND x 5"	AXLE
2	PC	1" DIAMETER	WHEELS
1	PC	1" x 1⅛" x 20"	VANE ARM
1	PC	¼" x 7" x 10"	VANE
2	PC	7¼" x 8½"	GLASS
2	PC	8¼" x 10½"	"
1	PC	3¼" x 6"	"
1	PC	8" TIN	PROPELLER
1	PC	¼" x 4" x 4"	METAL PLATE
1	BICYCLE HUB		
2	¼" BOLTS		
4	1" SCREWS		

"TROLLEY" FEEDER

BILL OF MATERIAL

1 PC	¾" x 6" x 11"	BOTTOM
1 PC	¾" x 10" x 8½"	PARTITION
2 PC	½" x 1¼" x 11"	SIDES
2 PC	½" x 1¼" x 5"	ENDS
2 PC	½" x 6" x 1¾"	GABLES
2 PC	½" x 4¾" x 13"	ROOF
2		MEAT HOLDERS
2		SCREW EYES

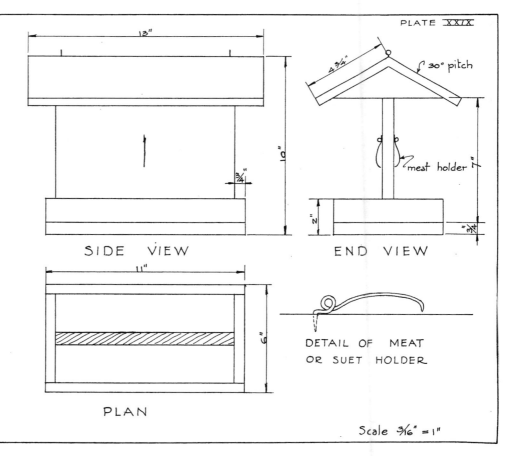

PLATE XXIX

SIDE VIEW

END VIEW

PLAN

DETAIL OF MEAT
OR SUET HOLDER

Scale ³⁄₁₆" = 1"

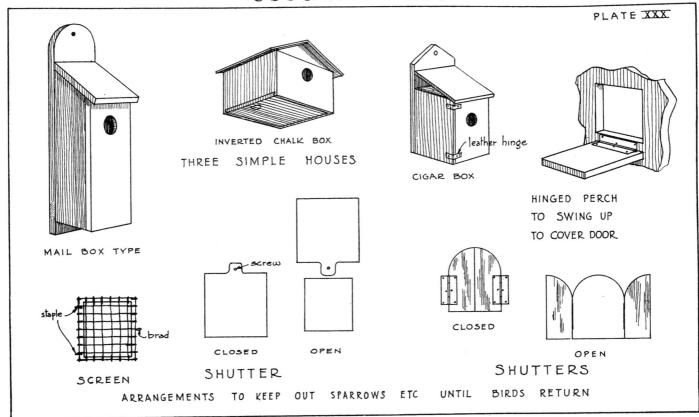

PLATE XXX

MAIL BOX TYPE

INVERTED CHALK BOX

THREE SIMPLE HOUSES

CIGAR BOX

leather hinge

HINGED PERCH
TO SWING UP
TO COVER DOOR

staple

brad

SCREEN

screw

CLOSED   OPEN

SHUTTER

CLOSED

OPEN

SHUTTERS

ARRANGEMENTS TO KEEP OUT SPARROWS ETC UNTIL BIRDS RETURN

The front and ends are of glass. On windy days, in winter, the birds can feed, protected from the wind. The feeder works like a weather vane and the back of the plane is away from the wind. The bicycle hub works on ball bearings, and a slight change in the direction of the wind causes the plane to move. The self-feeder is an advantage as it can be filled with ground feed and drops the food as it is consumed. Food can also be placed on the floor of the feeder. A forked stick on each side of the feeder holds the suet and makes the interior of the plane more natural. It takes only a short time for the birds to become accustomed to the feeder. They will visit it daily in the winter. The chickadees are especially fond of the aeroplane feeder and claim it as their own.

TROLLEY FEEDER

The trolley feeder is handy as it can be moved about. (Plate XXIX.) It can be placed on a wire or clothesline. The hooks, as shown in the drawing, are for holding the suet. The bottom of the feeder will hold considerable food, such as ground seeds and nuts. The birds soon become accustomed to this feeder and come to it without fear.

PERCH DESIGNS

PLATE XXXI

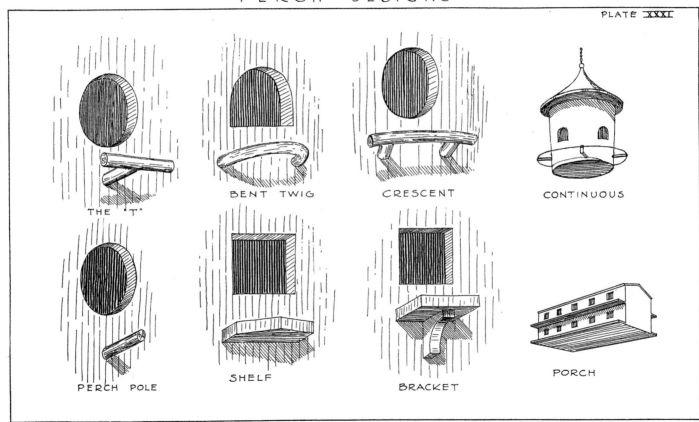

THE "T"

BENT TWIG

CRESCENT

CONTINUOUS

PERCH POLE

SHELF

BRACKET

PORCH

PLATE XXXII

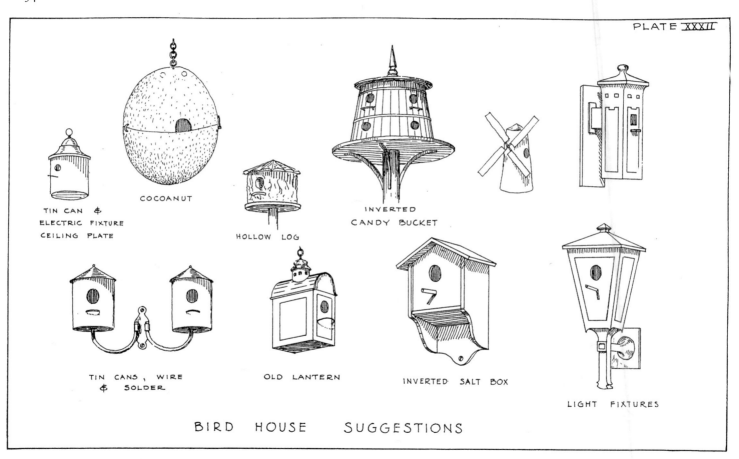

TIN CAN &
ELECTRIC FIXTURE
CEILING PLATE

COCOANUT

HOLLOW LOG

INVERTED
CANDY BUCKET

TIN CANS, WIRE
& SOLDER

OLD LANTERN

INVERTED SALT BOX

LIGHT FIXTURES

BIRD HOUSE SUGGESTIONS

SUGGESTIONS FOR HANGING AND PLACING BIRD HOUSES

PLATE XXXIII

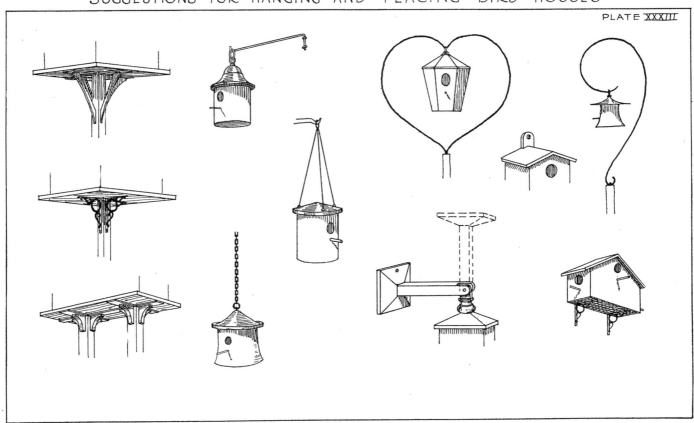

PLATE XXXIV

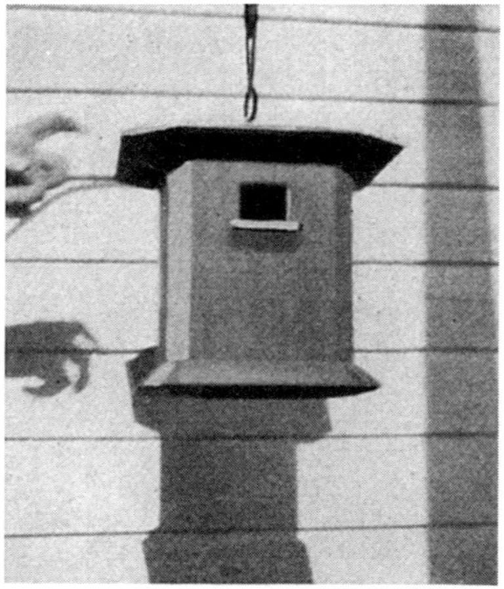

BLUE BIRD HOUSE

BILL OF MATERIAL

1	PC	3/4″ × 7½″ × 7½″	BOTTOM
2	PC.	3/4″ × 4½″ × 7″	FRONT & BACK
2	PC	3/4″ × 6″ × 7″	SIDES
1	PC	3/4″ × 9″ × 9″	TOP
1	PC	½″ × 2″ × 2″	CAP
1	PC	3/4″ × 3/4″ × 2″	PERCH
1	1″	RING AND SCREW EYE	
4	1½″	SCREWS	

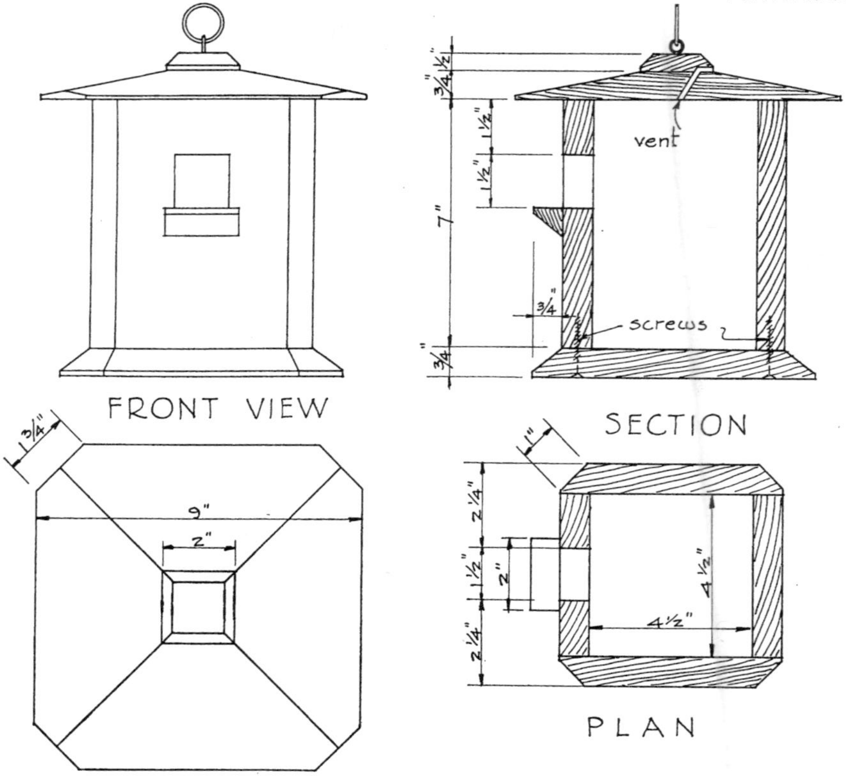
FRONT VIEW
SECTION
vent
screws
½″
3/4″
1½″
1½″
7″
3/4″
3/4″
TOP VIEW
3/4″
9″
2″
PLAN
1″
2¼″
1½″
2″
2¼″
4½″
4½″

Scale ▬ = 1″

EASY PROJECTS FOR BEGINNERS

A selection of easy-to-build birdhouses
specially designed for the novice woodworker.

BLUE BIRD HOUSE

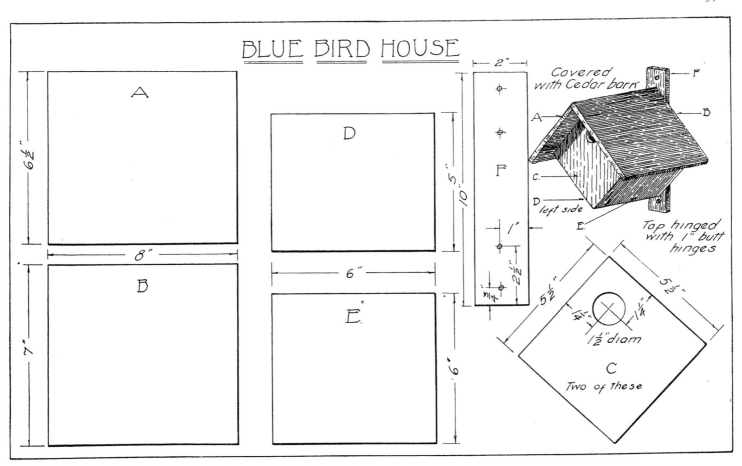

A

B

D

E

F

Covered with Cedar bark

left side

Top hinged with 1" butt hinges

1½" diam

C

Two of these

BLUE BIRD HOUSE.

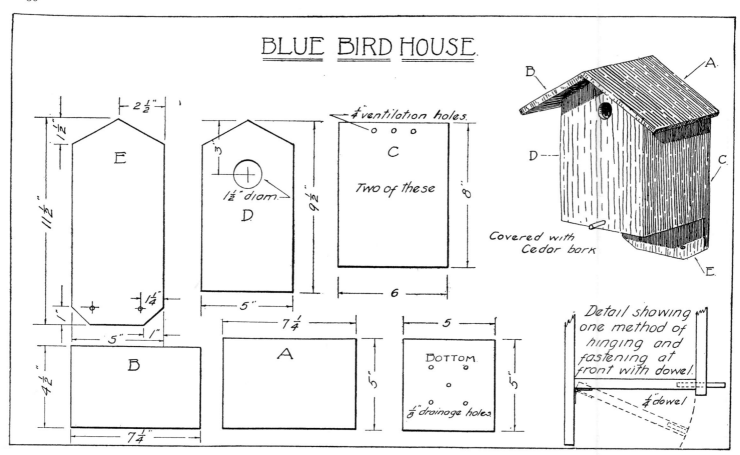

E

2½"

1½"

11¾"

1"

5"   1"

¼" ventilation holes.

o o o

C

Two of these

8"

6"

3"

1½" diam.

D

9½"

5"

B

4½"

7¼"

A

5"

7¼"

5

BOTTOM

⅛" drainage holes.

5"

Covered with
Cedar bark

B   A

D

C

E.

Detail showing
one method of
hinging and
fastening at
front with dowel.

¼" dowel

BLUE BIRD HOUSE

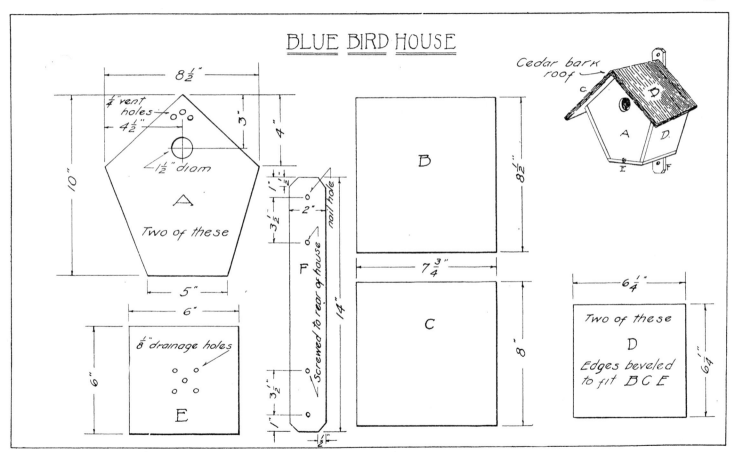

A Two of these

$8\frac{1}{2}"$

$\frac{1}{4}"$ vent holes

$4\frac{1}{2}"$

$1\frac{1}{2}"$ diam

$3"$

$4"$

$10"$

$5"$

Cedar bark roof

$6"$ drainage holes

$6"$

$6"$

E

$\frac{1}{8}"$

F Screwed to rear of house

nail hole

$1"$

$1\frac{1}{2}"$

$2"$

$3\frac{1}{2}"$

$14"$

$3\frac{1}{2}"$

$1"$

$\frac{1}{2}"$

B

C

$8\frac{1}{2}"$

$7\frac{3}{4}"$

$8"$

$6\frac{1}{4}"$

$6\frac{1}{4}"$

Two of these

D

Edges beveled to fit *B C E*

BLUE BIRD HOUSE

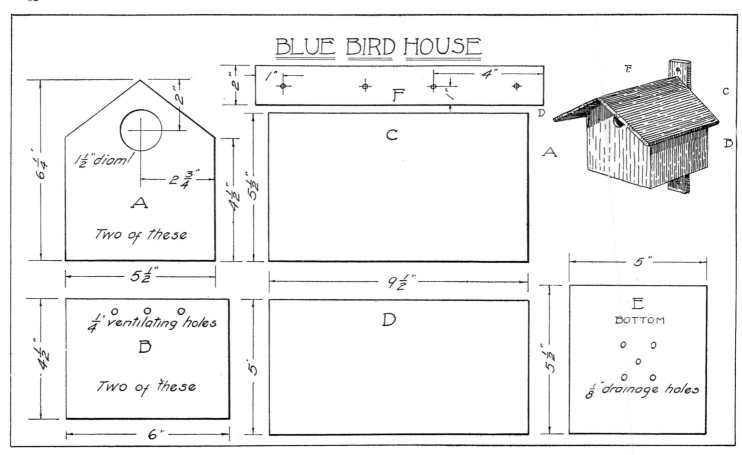

A — Two of these — $6\frac{1}{4}"$ — $5\frac{1}{2}"$ — $1\frac{1}{2}"diam!$ — $2\frac{3}{4}"$ — $2"$

F — $2"$ — $1"$ — $4"$

C — $4\frac{1}{2}"$ — $5\frac{1}{2}"$ — $9\frac{1}{2}"$

B — Two of these — $\frac{1}{4}"$ ventilating holes — $4\frac{1}{2}"$ — $6"$

D — $5"$ — $5\frac{1}{2}"$

E — BOTTOM — $\frac{1}{8}"$ drainage holes — $5"$

BLUE BIRD HOUSE

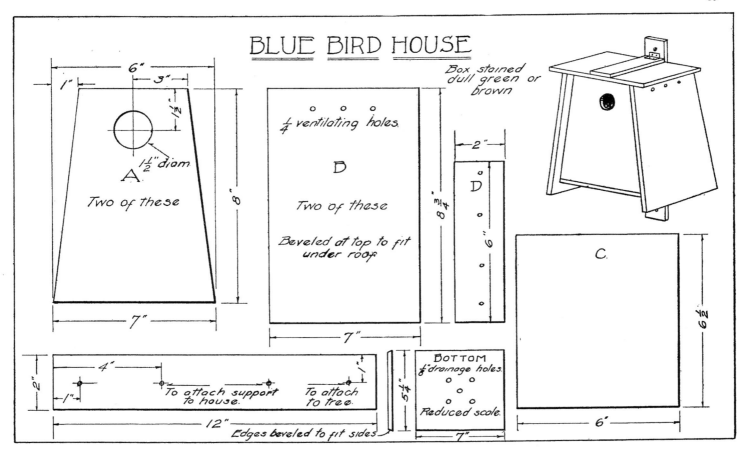

Box stained dull green or brown

6"
3"
1"
½"

1½" diam

A

Two of these

8"

7"

¼ ventilating holes

B

Two of these

Beveled at top to fit under roof

8¾"

7"

2"

D

6"

C

6½"

6'

4"
2"
1"
1"

To attach support to house.

To attach to tree.

12"

Edges beveled to fit sides

5¼"

BOTTOM
⅜ drainage holes.

Reduced scale.

7"

BOX FOR ROBINS.

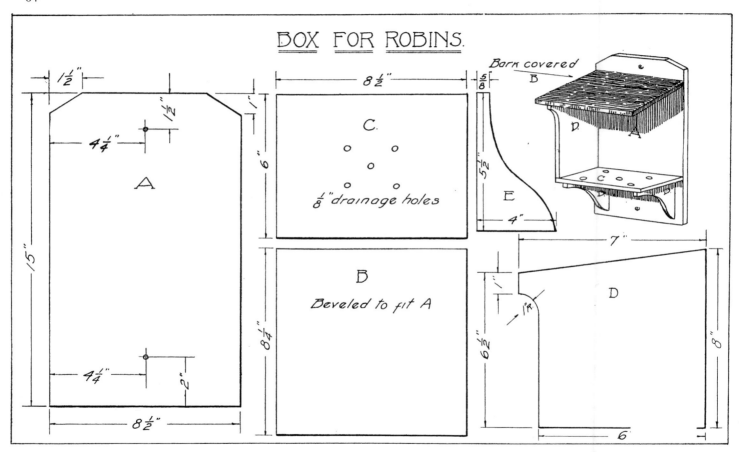

A

15"

1½"
½"
4¼"
4¼"
2"
8½"

C.

8½"
6"

⅛" drainage holes

B

Beveled to fit A

8¼"

E

⅝"
5½"
4"

Bark covered
B

D

C

A

D

7"
6½"
1"
8"
6

BOX FOR ROBINS.

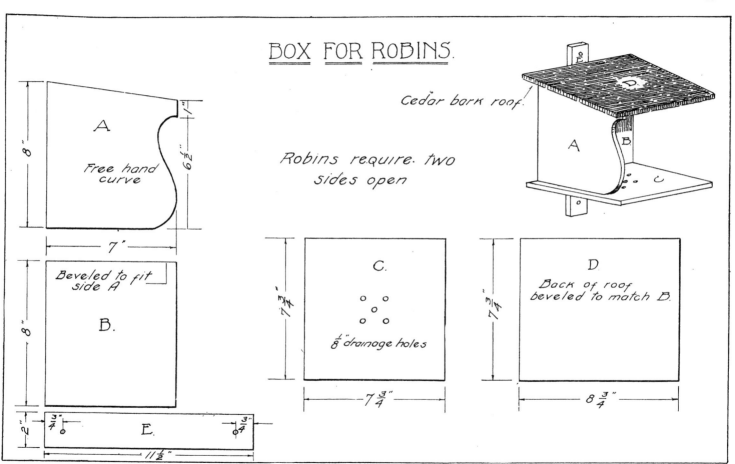

Cedar bark roof.

Robins require two
sides open

A
Free hand
curve

8"

6½"

1"

7"

Beveled to fit
side A

B.

8"

C.

7¾"

⅛" drainage holes

7¾"

D

Back of roof
beveled to match B.

7¾"

8¾"

E.

2"

¾"

¾"

11½"

BOX FOR WRENS.

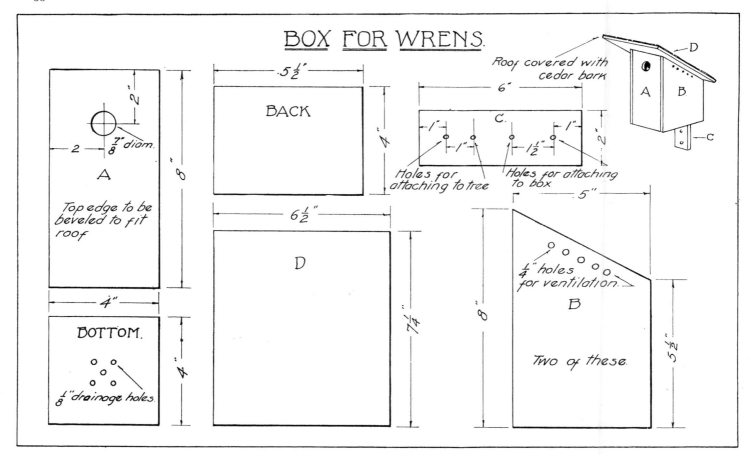

A — Top edge to be beveled to fit roof
2" — $\frac{7}{8}$" diam.
8"
4"

BOTTOM.
$\frac{1}{8}$" drainage holes.
4"

BACK — $5\frac{1}{2}$" — 4"

D — $6\frac{1}{2}$" — $7\frac{1}{4}$"

C. — 6" — 1" — 1" — $1\frac{1}{2}$" — 1" — 2"
Holes for attaching to tree
Holes for attaching to box

B — 5" — $\frac{1}{4}$" holes for ventilation — 8" — $5\frac{1}{2}$" — Two of these.

Roof covered with cedar bark
A B C D

67

DOUBLE WREN HOUSE.

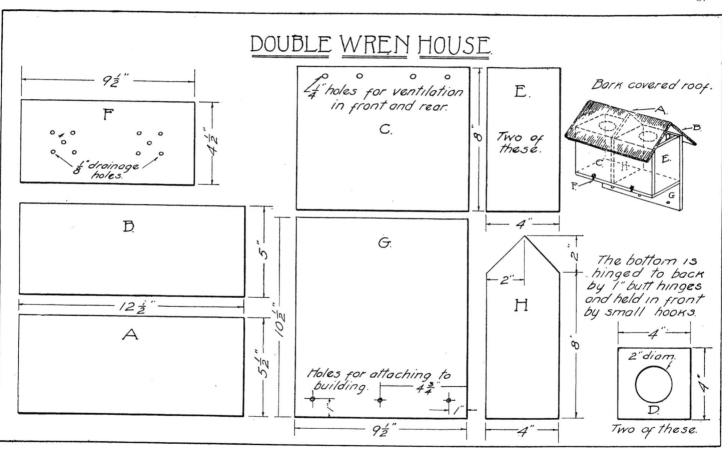

DOWNY WOODPECKER HOUSE

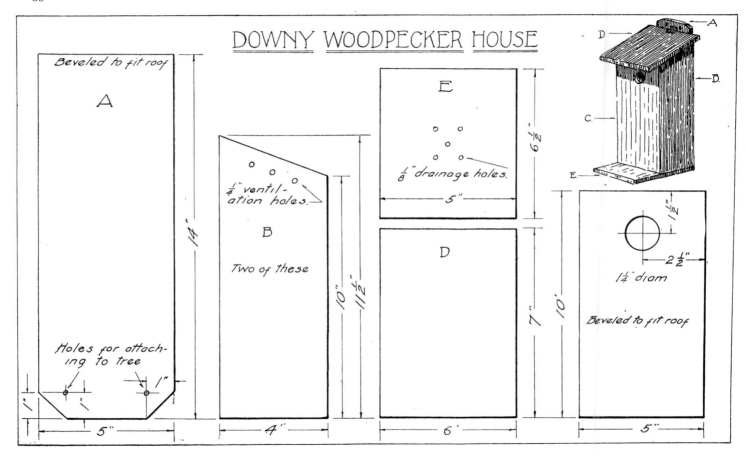

Beveled to fit roof

A

14"

Holes for attaching to tree

1"   1"   1"

5"

B

Two of these

$\frac{1}{4}$" ventilation holes.

10"   11$\frac{1}{2}$"

4"

E

$\frac{1}{8}$" drainage holes.

6$\frac{1}{2}$"

5"

D

7"   10'

6'

$\frac{1}{2}$"

2$\frac{1}{2}$"

1$\frac{1}{4}$" diam

Beveled to fit roof

5"

A   D   C   E

BOX FOR HAIRY WOODPECKERS.

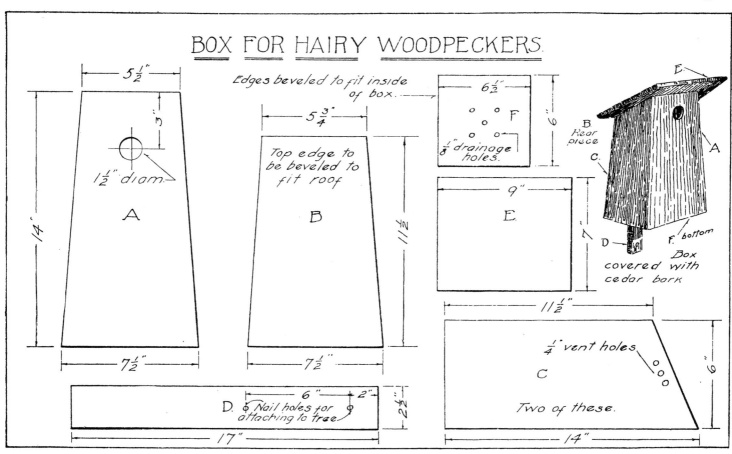

5½"

3"

1½" diam.

14"

A

7½"

Edges beveled to fit inside of box.

5¾"

Top edge to be beveled to fit roof

B

11½

7½"

6½"

F

⅛" drainage holes.

6"

9"

E

7"

B. Rear piece

C.

A

D

F. bottom

Box covered with cedar bark

E

6"

2½"

D. Nail holes for attaching to tree

17"

6" 2"

11½"

¼" vent holes

C

Two of these.

6"

14"

FLICKER HOUSE.

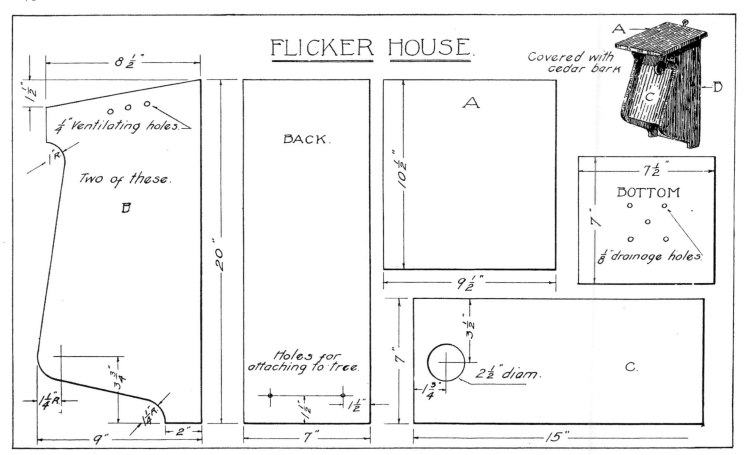

Covered with cedar bark

$\frac{1}{4}$" Ventilating holes.

8 $\frac{1}{2}$"

1 $\frac{1}{2}$"

1" R.

Two of these.

B

20"

3 $\frac{3}{4}$"

1 $\frac{1}{4}$ R.

$\frac{1}{4}$" R.

9"

2"

BACK.

Holes for attaching to tree.

7"

$\frac{1}{2}$"

1 $\frac{1}{2}$"

A

10 $\frac{1}{2}$"

9 $\frac{1}{2}$"

BOTTOM

7 $\frac{1}{2}$"

7"

$\frac{1}{8}$" drainage holes.

7"

3 $\frac{1}{2}$"

2 $\frac{1}{2}$" diam.

1 $\frac{3}{4}$"

C.

15"

WOODPECKER HOUSE

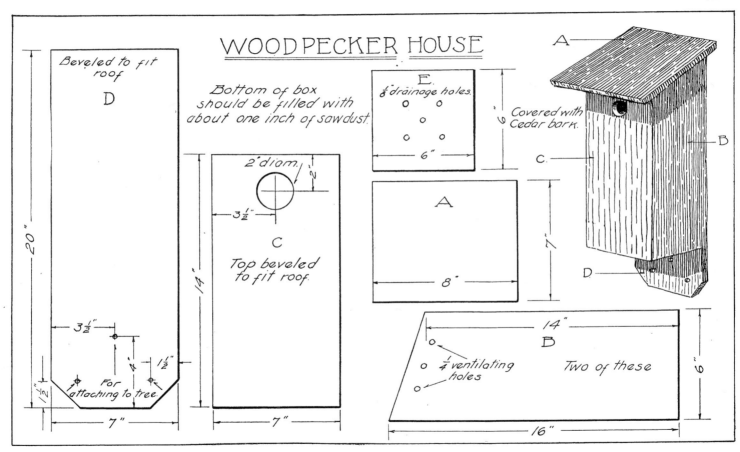

Beveled to fit roof

D

Bottom of box should be filled with about one inch of sawdust.

E.
$\frac{1}{8}$" drainage holes.

6"

6"

Covered with Cedar bark.

2" diam.

$3\frac{1}{2}$"

C

Top beveled to fit roof.

A

8"

7"

20"

14"

$3\frac{1}{2}$"

4"

$1\frac{1}{2}$"

$\frac{1}{2}$"

For attaching to tree.

7"

7"

A

B

C

D

14"

B

$\frac{1}{4}$" ventilating holes

Two of these

6"

16"

NUTHATCH HOUSE

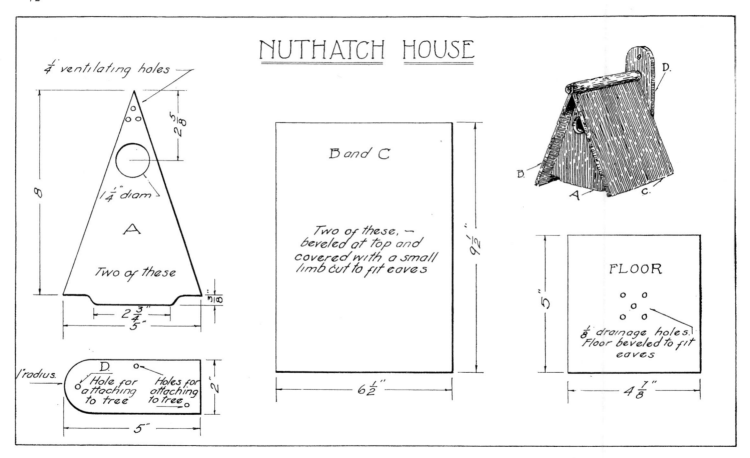

A — Two of these

$\frac{1}{4}"$ ventilating holes

$2\frac{5}{8}"$

$8"$

$1\frac{1}{4}"$ diam

$2\frac{3}{4}"$

$5"$

$\frac{3}{8}"$

B and C

Two of these, — beveled at top and covered with a small limb cut to fit eaves

$9\frac{1}{2}"$

$6\frac{1}{2}"$

D

Hole for attaching to tree

Holes for attaching to tree

1" radius.

$2"$

$5"$

FLOOR

$\frac{1}{8}"$ drainage holes. Floor beveled to fit eaves

$5"$

$4\frac{7}{8}"$

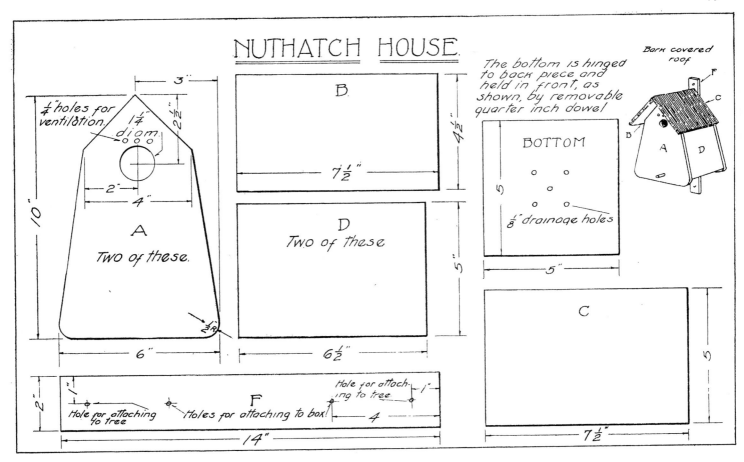

NUTHATCH HOUSE.

A — Two of these.

¼" holes for ventilation.

1¼" diam

3

2½"

10"

2"

4"

6"

⅜ R.

B

7½"

4½"

D — Two of these

6½"

The bottom is hinged to back piece and held in front, as shown, by removable quarter inch dowel

BOTTOM

⅛" drainage holes

5

5"

Bark covered roof

B
F
C
A
D

C

7½"

5

F

2"

1"

1"

Hole for attaching to tree

Holes for attaching to box

Hole for attaching to tree

4

14"

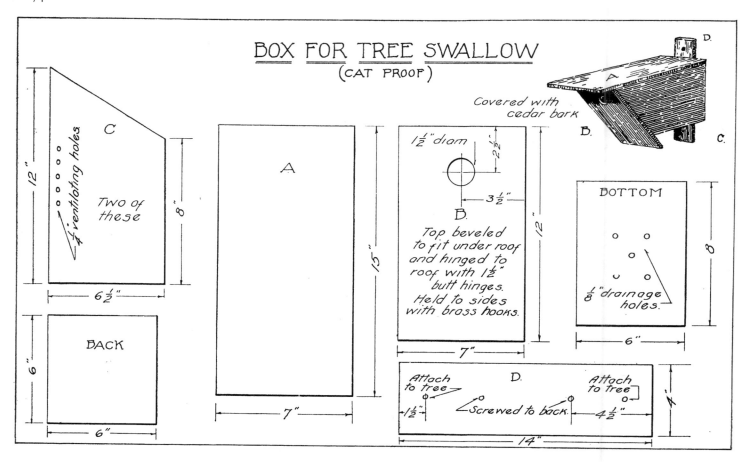

BOX FOR TREE SWALLOW
(CAT PROOF)

C — Two of these — $\frac{1}{4}$" ventilating holes — 12" — 8" — $6\frac{1}{2}$"

BACK — 6" — 6"

A — 15" — 7"

Covered with cedar bark

$1\frac{1}{2}$" diam — $2\frac{1}{2}$" — $3\frac{1}{2}$" — B. — Top beveled to fit under roof and hinged to roof with $1\frac{1}{2}$" butt hinges. Held to sides with brass hooks. — 12" — 7"

BOTTOM — $\frac{1}{8}$" drainage holes. — 8" — 6"

D. — Attach to tree — Attach to tree — Screwed to back — $1\frac{1}{2}$" — $4\frac{1}{2}$" — 4" — 14"

TITMOUSE HOUSE

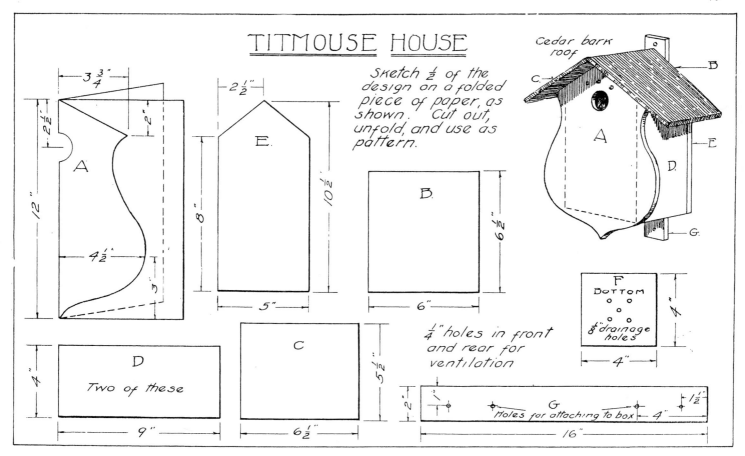

Sketch ½ of the design on a folded piece of paper, as shown. Cut out, unfold, and use as pattern.

Cedar bark roof

A

12"

2½"

3¾"

2"

4½"

3"

E

2½"

8"

10½"

5"

B

6½"

6"

D

Two of these

4"

9"

C

5½"

6½"

¼" holes in front and rear for ventilation

F

BOTTOM

⅛" drainage holes

4"

4"

G

1"

2"

Holes for attaching to box

1½"

4"

16"

CHICKADEE HOUSE.

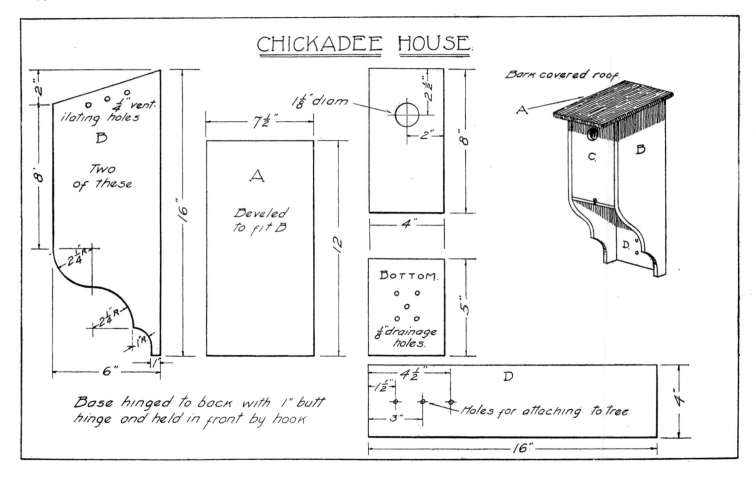

2"

$\frac{1}{4}$" vent-
ilating holes

B

Two
of these

16"

$2\frac{1}{4}$ R.

$2\frac{1}{4}$ R.

1" R.

6"

1"

Base hinged to back with 1" butt
hinge and held in front by hook

7$\frac{1}{2}$"

A

Beveled
to fit B

12

1$\frac{1}{8}$" diam

2$\frac{1}{2}$"

2"

8"

4"

Bottom.

$\frac{1}{8}$" drainage
holes.

5"

Bark covered roof.

A

C

B

D.

4$\frac{1}{2}$"

1$\frac{1}{2}$"

D

3"

Holes for attaching to tree

16"

4"

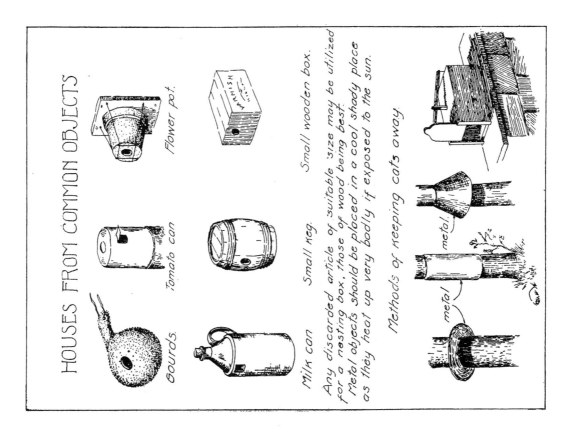

HOUSES FROM COMMON OBJECTS

Flower pot.

Small wooden box.

Tomato can

Small keg.

Gourds.

Milk can

Any discarded article of suitable size may be utilized for a nesting box, those of wood being best. Metal objects should be placed in a cool shady place as they heat up very badly if exposed to the sun.

Methods of keeping cats away.

metal.

metal.

78

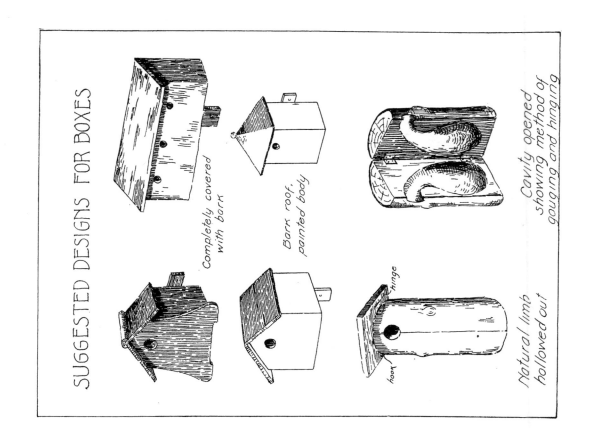

SUGGESTED DESIGNS FOR BOXES

Completely covered with bark

Bark roof, painted body

Cavity opened showing method of gouging and hinging

hinge

hook

Natural limb hollowed out

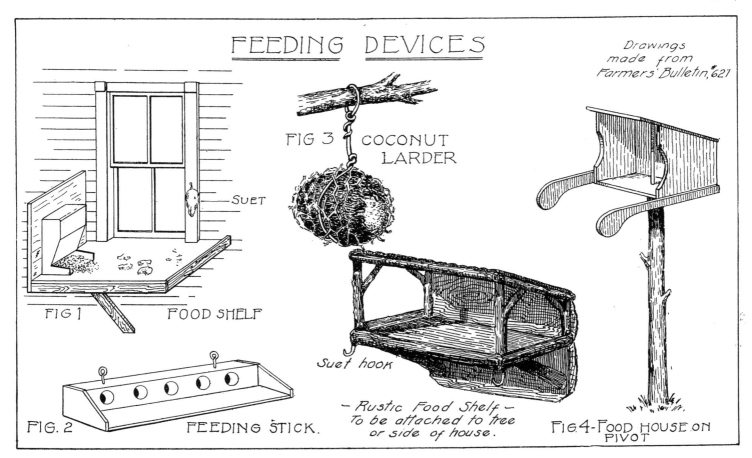

FEEDING DEVICES

Drawings
made from
Farmers' Bulletin, 621

SUET

FIG 1 — FOOD SHELF

FIG 3 COCONUT LARDER

Suet hook

FIG. 2 — FEEDING STICK.

— Rustic Food Shelf —
To be attached to tree
or side of house.

FIG 4 — FOOD HOUSE ON PIVOT